Unreal Development Kit
Beginner's Guide

A fun, quick, step-by-step guide to level design and creating your own game world

Richard Moore

PUBLISHING

BIRMINGHAM - MUMBAI

Unreal Development Kit
Beginner's Guide

First published: August 2011

Production Reference: 2090212

Published by Packt Publishing Ltd.
Livery Place
35 Livery Street
Birmingham B3 2PB, UK.

ISBN 978-1-849690-52-2

www.packtpub.com

Cover Image by Richard Moore (rich.2bdigital@yahoo.co.uk)

Credits

Author

Richard J Moore

Reviewers

Taylor Paschal

Jamie Telford

Dave Voyles

Patrick Coan

Acquisition Editor

Steven Wilding

Development Editor

Meeta Rajani

Technical Editor

Lubna Shaikh

Copy Editor

Laxmi Subramanian

Project Coordinator

Leena Purkait

Proofreader

Samantha Lyon

Indexer

Tejal Daruwale

Production Coordinator

Alwin Roy

Cover Work

Alwin Roy

About the Author

Richard J Moore graduated in 2009 with a degree in video games design from Hull School of Art and Design, but has expanded his creativity by working as a web designer/illustrator in Hull, East Yorkshire, and London for three years. He is very passionate about 3D modeling, level design, concept drawing, web development, and graphical illustrations.

He has worked on a number of different projects with clients from different industrial backgrounds, building an impressive collection of stylish web templates, logos, brochures, business cards, web banners, animated graphics, and e-mail marketing campaigns.

Through the clouds lies his passion for video game development, complete creation of 3D art including modeling, texturing and high resolution rendering. He also dazzles in game documentation and conceptual drawings.

He will always take any opportunity to meet as many different people from the game development community as possible, and as a result he has attended the Games Grads career fair, participated in the Game Republic 2009 student showcase in Sheffield and Platform 2010, Hull's 1st Digital and Gaming event where he won the award for best character and a cheque for £100.

In March 2011, he was involved in Platform Expo's 2011, Hull's second video game expo where he entered in this year's video game showcase and won 2nd prize for his outstanding contribution to video game design and is now involved in Platform Expo's 2012.

In July 2011, he volunteered as a marketing assistant/designer for an online-based video games magazine, assisting the editor-in-chief in designing templates for latest issues of the magazine, writing reviews on the latest video game titles, and talking to clients about potential advertising coverage within the magazine and online. In his spare time he focuses on freelance design and development work with upcoming companies. As a result, Richard has had some impressive feedback from fellow designers and clients, and is very much interested in starting up his very own design company, focusing on all the things he loves. He has the ideas, the drive, and determination to put it together. 2011 is the start of something big for this video games designer.

I would like to thank all the people at Packt Publishing for producing this book and allowing me to take part in writing this creative guide to the Unreal Development Kit.

I would also like to thank the people at Epic Games for allowing me, as a games designer, to create fantastic 3D environments and brand new game ideas using their engine.

(Cheers, all I need from you now is a job position.)

Finally, I'd like to thank the people at Adobe, Autodesk, and Pixologic for letting me show my creativity in creating some amazing game design artwork, using your software.

(Keep up the good work.)

About the Reviewers

Taylor Paschal grew up surrounded by video games. As the game industry skyrocketed in the mid-nineties, games like GoldenEye and Zelda consumed his time. Inspired by the beautiful environments of the games he played, Taylor constantly dreamt of one day being able to entertain others with levels made by his own design. That dream never left him.

Now over a decade later, Taylor is a senior, expected to graduate from Radford University in May 2011 with a degree in Software Engineering. Specializing in game development practices and level design, he works with an upcoming studio of talented individuals, overseeing the art and level design of their games, which make use of the Mobile UDK. In his spare time, he does graphic design work, creating logos, ads, and wallpapers on request.

Taylor has over three years of experience with the Unreal 3 Engine. Meeting with developers from Epic Games to enhance his knowledge of the engine and attending game development conferences to learn about level design theory, Taylor applies his much sought-after skills to his work, creating vibrant and exciting worlds for players to explore.

I want to thank Andrew Bains and Demond Rogers at Epic Games for being great teachers and a great source of inspiration for me. I also want to thank Alex Meade and Austin De Vinney for convincing me to go to that first game developer's conference. I don't think I'd be pursuing a career in level design if it weren't for that trip. Also a shout out to Alex Meade (again) and Matt Varnell, for helping me make some awesome games in the Mobile UDK, as well as Michael Thola for letting us test on his iPad. Dr. Jeff Pittges, too, for giving me the confidence to network myself in the games industry. Last, and definitely the most important, my family. I wouldn't be here if it weren't for your patience and your help, so thank you Mom, Dad, James, Cody, Michaela, and Julie.

Jamie Telford is a Technical Artist in the field of real-time applications and game development. His primary expertise is in developing robust animation systems for deployment in modern cutting edge software applications.

Jamie's years of experience in the games and education industry have given him an excellent insight into current and upcoming methodology and techniques deployed in successful development environments.

He has worked for Fuzzyeyes Studio and Ksatria Gameworks as an animator and rigger. In addition to his industry experience, he has worked for several years as a lecturer in animation and modeling for Ngee Ann Polytechnic of Singapore.

Minazo, the walrus

Dave Voyles is Managing Editor and Podcast Producer for Armless Octopus. He covers Xbox Live Indie Game, Xbox Live Arcade, and Playstation Network news, reviews, and developer interviews. He holds a B.S. in Communication Studies from SUNY Oneonta, and is currently attending the New York Institute of Technology to work on his MBA in Management of Information Systems.

Dave also builds projects focusing on the Unreal Development Kit. Most notably, he is founder of the New York City-based UDK meetup group, where he works with other developers to collaborate on endeavors in a physical environment, as well as provides tutorials. He is currently developing a third-person adventure title of his own, and plans to release it on the PC later this year.

You can find more of his work by visiting his site at `http://www.DaveVoyles.wordpress.com` or `www.ArmlessOctopus.com`.

www.PacktPub.com

Support files, eBooks, discount offers and more

You might want to visit www.PacktPub.com for support files and downloads related to your book.

Did you know that Packt offers eBook versions of every book published, with PDF and ePub files available? You can upgrade to the eBook version at www.PacktPub.com and as a print book customer, you are entitled to a discount on the eBook copy. Get in touch with us at service@packtpub.com for more details.

At www.PacktPub.com, you can also read a collection of free technical articles, sign up for a range of free newsletters and receive exclusive discounts and offers on Packt books and eBooks.

http://PacktLib.PacktPub.com

Do you need instant solutions to your IT questions? PacktLib is Packt's online digital book library. Here, you can access, read and search across Packt's entire library of books.

Why Subscribe?

- ◆ Fully searchable across every book published by Packt
- ◆ Copy and paste, print and bookmark content
- ◆ On demand and accessible via web browser

Free Access for Packt account holders

If you have an account with Packt at www.PacktPub.com, you can use this to access PacktLib today and view nine entirely free books. Simply use your login credentials for immediate access.

This book is dedicated to:

My parents, Elizabeth and John, who taught me all that is important,

my brother Adam, and my sister Sarah who taught me to never give up, and

finally to all my relatives, friends and fellow games designers.

This book would not have been possible without your love and understanding.

Thank you from the bottom of my heart.

(I'll make it up to you all, I promise.)

Table of Contents

Preface

UDK offers a fully integrated editing environment through the renowned Unreal Editor. You will learn all of the engine's key tools which are accessible through Unreal Editor. You will learn the basics, from installing to navigating around the editor. You will then start putting together your first level using step-by-step instructions.

You will then learn how to use UDK's real world features, such as dynamic lighting and shadows, particle effects, physics, terrain, item placement, and advanced AI/bot pathing.

Finally, you will learn about UDK's cutting edge high level scripting, adding materials followed by some advanced techniques to boost your skills as a designer, and look beyond UDK with further development into external content, unreal scripting, and modding.

What this book covers

Chapter 1, Level Design HQ will explain how to download and install UDK. It will show you how to launch the editor, how to move and rotate around the editor, and finally explain briefly about BSP brushes and static meshes.

Chapter 2, Hello UDK covers the most essential tools and functions you need to know to get started with UDK. You'll be able to quickly jump into UDK and begin feeling comfortable using the most commonly used functions.

Chapter 3, Applying Lighting Effects covers the different types of lighting used in developing and designing an environment in UDK, and how light maps are used on CSG surfaces and static meshes to reflect light off objects.

Chapter 4, Battling the Elements looks at UDK's particle editor (Cascade) works. It will quickly walk you through the interface of the editor and explain how a basic smoke particle, water, height, and fog can be set up.

Chapter 5, Movement with Movers introduces you to the world of animated level geometry in UDK, doors, and elevators, which are activated using InterpActors or triggers.

Chapter 6, Terrain will explain the reader how to set up and modify terrain in UDK.

Chapter 7, Adding Gameplay Elements into your Map explains how to get all of the basic gameplay elements into your map. In this section, we'll set up a Deathmatch map, which is the easiest type to create.

Chapter 8, Complex Event Sequences introduces the reader to UIScenes, for creation of HUD elements, menus, and things like subtitles and titles.

Chapter 9, Materials will explain the basics of creating a material. We'll build some basic (but extremely useful) materials from scratch, and in the process, learn how the material editor works.

What you need for this book

You will need the latest version of Unreal Development Kit.

System requirements:

- ◆ Minimum:
    - ❑ Windows XP SP2 or Windows Vista
    - ❑ 2.0+ GHz processor
    - ❑ 2 GB system RAM
    - ❑ SM3-compatible video card
    - ❑ 3 GB free hard drive space

- ◆ Recommended for Content Development:
    - ❑ Windows 7 64-bit
    - ❑ 2.0+ GHz multi-core processor
    - ❑ 8 GB System RAM
    - ❑ NVIDIA 8000 series or higher graphics card
    - ❑ Plenty of free hard drive space

- ◆ Minimum for DX11 Development:
    - ❑ Windows Vista
    - ❑ 2.0+ GHz processor
    - ❑ 2 GB system RAM
    - ❑ DX11 Graphics Card such as Nvidia: 400 series or above and ATI: 5000 series or above
    - ○ 3 GB free hard drive space

Who this book is for

This book is for aspiring game developers who want to learn how to create their own levels, maps, game worlds, and environments. You don't need game design or game development experience, and no experience of UDK is required

Conventions

In this book, you will find several headings appearing frequently.

To give clear instructions of how to complete a procedure or task, we use:

Time for action – heading

1. Action 1
2. Action 2
3. Action 3

Instructions often need some extra explanation so that they make sense, so they are followed with:

What just happened?

This heading explains the working of tasks or instructions that you have just completed.

You will also find some other learning aids in the book, including:

Pop quiz – heading

These are short multiple choice questions intended to help you test your own understanding.

Have a go hero – heading

These set practical challenges and give you ideas for experimenting with what you have learned.

You will also find a number of styles of text that distinguish between different kinds of information. Here are some examples of these styles, and an explanation of their meaning.

New terms and **important words** are shown in bold. Words that you see on the screen, in menus or dialog boxes for example, appear in the text like this: "To launch the unreal editor, go to the **Start Menu | Unreal Development Kit | UDK Version | Editor**".

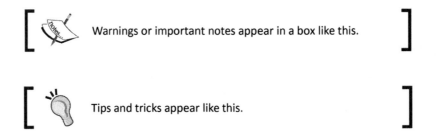

Warnings or important notes appear in a box like this.

Tips and tricks appear like this.

Reader feedback

Feedback from our readers is always welcome. Let us know what you think about this book—what you liked or may have disliked. Reader feedback is important for us to develop titles that you really get the most out of.

To send us general feedback, simply send an e-mail to feedback@packtpub.com, and mention the book title via the subject of your message.

If there is a book that you need and would like to see us publish, please send us a note in the **SUGGEST A TITLE** form on www.packtpub.com or e-mail suggest@packtpub.com.

If there is a topic that you have expertise in and you are interested in either writing or contributing to a book, see our author guide on www.packtpub.com/authors.

Customer support

Now that you are the proud owner of a Packt book, we have a number of things to help you to get the most from your purchase.

Errata

Although we have taken every care to ensure the accuracy of our content, mistakes do happen. If you find a mistake in one of our books—maybe a mistake in the text or the code—we would be grateful if you would report this to us. By doing so, you can save other readers from frustration and help us improve subsequent versions of this book. If you find any errata, please report them by visiting http://www.packtpub.com/support, selecting your book, clicking on the **errata submission form** link, and entering the details of your errata. Once your errata are verified, your submission will be accepted and the errata will be uploaded on our website, or added to any list of existing errata, under the Errata section of that title. Any existing errata can be viewed by selecting your title from http://www.packtpub.com/support.

Piracy

Piracy of copyright material on the Internet is an ongoing problem across all media. At Packt, we take the protection of our copyright and licenses very seriously. If you come across any illegal copies of our works, in any form, on the Internet, please provide us with the location address or website name immediately so that we can pursue a remedy.

Please contact us at copyright@packtpub.com with a link to the suspected pirated material.

We appreciate your help in protecting our authors, and our ability to bring you valuable content.

Questions

You can contact us at questions@packtpub.com if you are having a problem with any aspect of the book, and we will do our best to address it.

1
Level Design HQ

*In the first chapter, I'm going to explain how to download and install the **Unreal Development Kit** (**UDK**), show you how to launch the editor, how to move and rotate around the editor, and finally briefly explain **Binary Space Partitioning** (**BSP**) brushes and static meshes.*

In this chapter, we will learn the following:

◆ UDK download and installation

◆ Launching the editor

◆ Movement and rotation

◆ Using BSP brushes and static meshes

So let's get on with it. We will first look at downloading the UDK, and install it on your PC.

Time for action – UDK download and installation

1. Download the latest version of UDK.

2. Log on to www.udk.com and download the latest version of unreal development kit beta. Once you download the UDK Installer, go ahead and install the UDK. The default directory for installing UDK is C:\UDK\UDK-VersionRelease.

Version Release will be the month and year that the UDK you downloaded was built.

UDK folder structure

The UDK folder structure looks like the following screenshot:

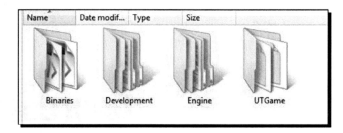

The UDK folder structure consists of the following four folders:

1. **Binaries**: game/binary executable.

2. **Development**: source code for UDK.

3. **Engine**: engine files.

4. **UTGame**: game files. For level-design and environment creation, the important folder here is the `content` folder. The packaged environment's assets such as models, textures, materials, sounds, and such are stored here.

   For environment creation and level design, the most important folder is **UTGame | Content | Environments**. It contains all the files you need to create your map, as shown in the following screenshot:

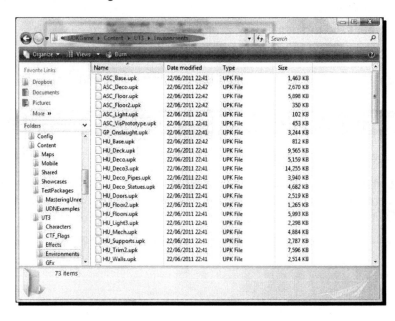

UDK extension is the UDK package's name. This is how the models and textures are stored in UDK. Think of UDK extension as folders. Inside those folders are stored all the models, animations, textures, materials, and similar assets. You can browse the UDK files through the UDK editor.

UDK is the map file extension.

Time for action – launching the editor

1. To launch the unreal editor, go to the **Start Menu | Unreal Development Kit | UDK Version | Editor**.

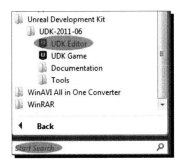

2. Another way to launch the editor is to create a shortcut. To do this, go to the installation folder: \UDK\UDK-VersionRelease\Binaries, locate UDKLift. exe, right-click and select **Send To | Desktop (create shortcut)**, as shown in the following screenshot:

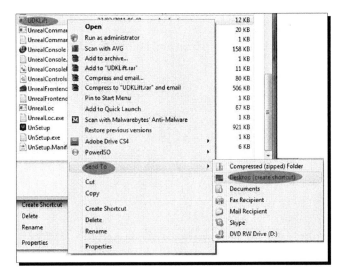

3. Once on you have created the shortcut on your desktop, right-click the shortcut and select **Properties**. Then, in the **Target** box under the **Shortcut** tab, **add** `editor` at the end of the text. It should look something like the following screenshot:

4. Now double-click on the desktop icon and launch the **UDK Editor**.

Autosave

When you first launch the editor, you will have Autosave automatically enabled. This will save your map at a chosen timed interval. You can set how often it will automatically save by clicking the **Left Mouse Button (LMB)** on the arrow on the bottom-right of the **Autosave Interval** and choosing the time you want, as shown in the following screenshot:

You will find the Autosave feature at the bottom right of the editor. If you enable Autosave, there are a few options such as **Interval** and **Type**.

Save manually by going up to **File | Save As**.

Content browser

Content browser is where you will find off the game's assets. Placing static meshes (models), textures, sounds, and game entities such as player starts, weapons, and so on, can all be done through the content browser. You will be using the content browser very often. To open the content browser click on the top menu bar, as shown in the following screenshot:

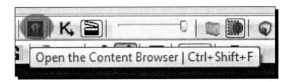

Packages are where you will find specific items contained within the UDK. Things such as static meshes are contained within a package. You can search for a package, or just find the package you want to use and select it as shown in the following screenshot:

The top of the content browser contains a search box as well as a filter box. This is very useful. You can sort out the content in the browser by animation sets, material instances, static meshes, sounds, and so on. This helps a lot when looking for items. The next screenshot lists full names of the items within a selected package. You can sort by clicking on the **Name, Type**, **Tags**, or **Path fields**, and it will re-arrange the content's preview:

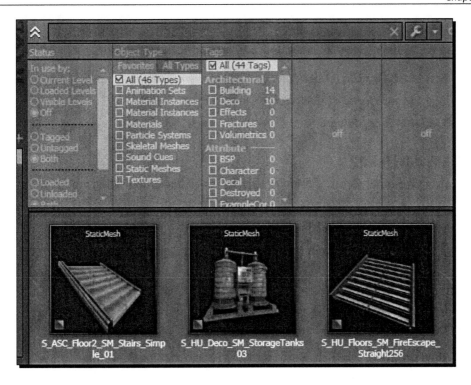

The content browser is one of the most commonly used tools in UDK. Get comfortable using the content browser. Spend some time navigating around it. UDK basics covers the most essential tools and functions you need to know to get started with UDK. You'll be able to quickly jump into UDK and begin feeling comfortable using the most commonly used functions.

What just happened?

So we know how to launch the editor, how to use the Autosave function, and where to find the content browser. We are now going to look at how to move and rotate around the editor.

Time for action – movement and rotation

Time to have a look at movement, rotation, and navigating around the editor.

Navigation

Buttons used to navigate around UDK.

UDK

These are your primary keys for navigating and rotating using the editor:

- **Left Mouse Button (LMB)**: pan right/left/forward/backward movements
- **Right Mouse Button (RMB)**: rotate, look around
- **LMB+RMB**: up/down

WASD key navigation

The following are other forms of primary keys for navigating and rotating around the editor:

- Click and hold RMB. As you hold it, use the *WASD* keyboard keys to move around as you would in a first person shooter game.
- *WASD* movement is great if you are familiar with hammer source mapping.

MAYA users

If you are familiar with Maya, the following will be your primary keys for navigating and rotating around the editor.

- Hold down the *U* key
- *U+ LMB*: rotate, look around
- *U+ RMB*: forward/backward movements
- *U+ MMB*: right/left/up/down movements

What just happened?

Now that you have installed UDK and know what the content browser is, you are ready to begin. So let's get started.

BSP

The purpose of BSP is to greatly reduce the amount of work the game engine has to perform in real time—to draw polygons on the player's screen.

Why use BSP?

BSP is a great tool to block in your map with. BSP is often used to quickly create and test playable space.

Can I use static meshes to create my map without using BSP?

Yes. Although, you will need a 3D software application that supports UDK's plug-in, such as Autodesk Maya, 3Ds Max, XSI.

UDK CSG Operations for Brushes include the following:

- CSG Add
- CSG Subtract
- CSG Intersect
- CSG Deintersect

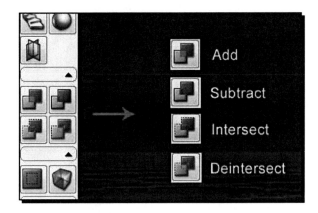

Dominance of static meshes

Static meshes are simply the models in your level. If you open up any UDK map, 90 percent of the map will be static meshes and the rest will be BSP brushes.

Brushes only, no static meshes

We can see only brushes used in the following image:

Brushes and static meshes

We can see both brushes and static meshes used in the following image:

Time for action – using BSP brushes and static meshes

The **Red Builder Brush** creates BSP brushes. It also acts as a template for creating **BSP Geometry** and does not show up in the game.

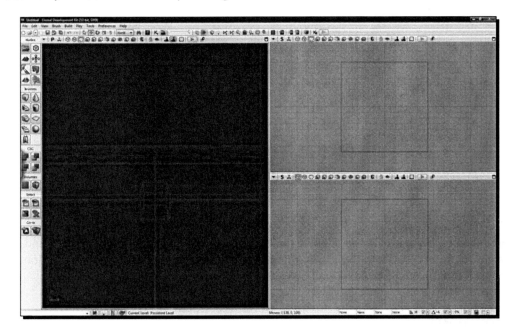

In the previous screenshot you can see that the red builder brush has taken the form of a square template for creating BSP geometry. You can create different sizes and types of BSP.

Hammer source engine still uses **BSP operation** to construct the main shell of the level, but the majority of next-gen engines heavily rely on static meshes. Static meshes is what you will be using to primarily define how your map looks in UDK. Static meshes are the models that make up the 90 percent of your level. Creating static meshes requires you to have a 3D application, such as XSI, Maya or 3Ds Max, and so on.

- Red builder brush is what you will use to create BSP brushes
- Static meshes is what you'll be using to detail the environment

Additive and subtractive

When you create a new map by going to **File | New**, you are presented with two options to create a map inside UDK: additive and subtractive. The most common and mostly used is the **Additive** mode.

Additive

Think of an empty space. In the additive method, you would be adding walls, models, and the environment assets into the empty space. A real life example of additive map creation would be constructing a building wall-by-wall.

Subtractive

Think of a solid rock. In the subtractive method, you would be cutting the rooms and environment out of this solid mass. Subtracting the solid rock, in order to have room, is like sculpting.

UDK basics covers the most essential tools and functions you need to know to get started with UDK. You'll be able to quickly jump into UDK and begin feeling comfortable using the most commonly used functions.

Unreal scale and proportions

The scale of a character in Unreal is 96 units.

- 128 UU = 8 feet = 243.8 cm
- 96 UU = 6 feet = 182.9 cm
- 16 UU = 1 foot = 30.5 cm
- 1 UU = 2 cm

Grid snapping

Grid snapping is extremely important. Always work with grid snaps turned on. There are three grid snap options: **rotation grid, drag grid,** and **scale grid**. The following screenshot shows the **Drag** grid option, the **Rotation** grid option, and the **Scale** grid option at the bottom-right corner:

Uncheck/check: turns on/off the drag/rotation/scale grids. I would recommend always having this turned on. In some cases, for fine detailed work, you may need to turn it off.

 [ ] Bracket keys increase or decrease grid.

Viewport options

The most commonly used viewport is **perspective**. You will spend most of your time in the perspective viewport. This includes moving, placing, duplicating, and transformation of static meshes and most of your environment creation.

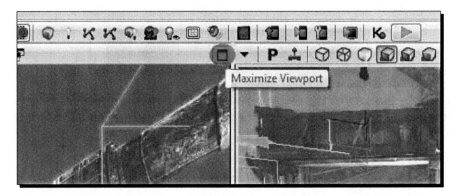

If you go up to **View | Viewport Configuration**, you have options of how you want to set up your views, which is shown in the following screenshot:

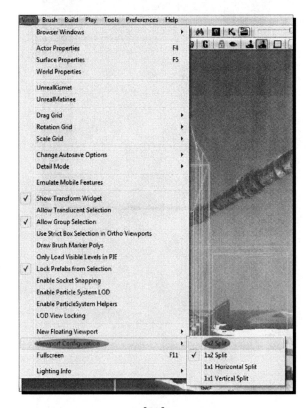

In the drop-down menu for the viewport, there are options of what you want to display. It allows you to hide/unhide specific elements in your perspective viewport, which is very useful when you are working on a specific element during your level creation:

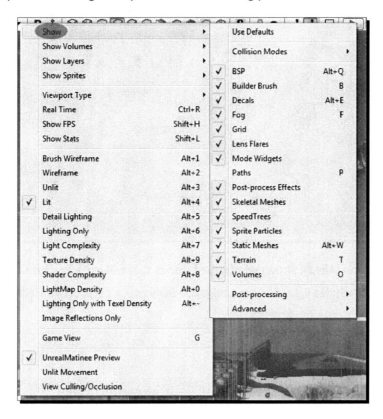

Real Time Preview (RTP) shows the environment as it would look like in the game, complete with sound and particle effects. RTP works best when you have the **Game Mode (G)** enabled, which turns off the **wireframe brush view**. This offers the best and most accurate view of what your level will look like in the game.

Here is a list of the different viewport options you will be using when designing in UDK. Some of you will use one more than the others:

◆ **Brush wireframe** (*Alt+1*): Shows wireframe brushes that will allow brush selection

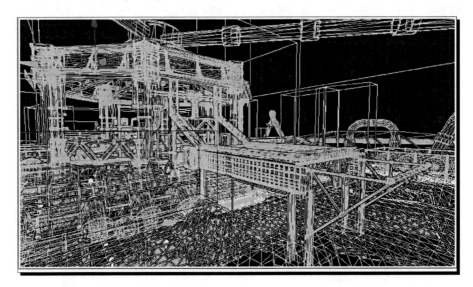

◆ **Wireframe** (*Alt+2*): Shows wireframe brushes that will not allow brush selection

◆ **Unlit** (*Alt+3*): No lights; makes navigation inside your perspective viewport a bit faster

◆ **Lit** (*Alt+4*): Full-lights preview

◆ **Lighting only** (*Alt+5*): Lighting only

- **Lighting complexity** (*Alt+6*): Your lighting complexity
- **Texture density** (*Alt+7*): How complex are your textures
- **Shader complexity** (*Alt+8*): Shader complexity only
- **Lightmap density** (*Alt+9*): Lightmap density only
- **Lighting only with texel density** (*Alt+0*): Lighting only with texel density

What just happened?

So we know about using the BSP brushes and static meshes, the additive and subtractive tools, the unreal scale and proportions, the grid snapping, and the different types of viewport options that we will be using when designing in UDK.

Have a go hero – wireframe brush

So we have light in our small room, what's next? Let's see if you can move the wireframe brush and create another surface. It is important that you understand the different uses of the translation and scaling mode options available in this editor.

Pop quiz

What do the following buttons function as?

- **Left Mouse Button (LMB)**
- **Right Mouse Button (RMB)**
- *LMB+RMB*
- *WASD*

Summary

So we have covered the UDK basics, which are the most essential tools and functions you need to know to get started with UDK. You'll be able to quickly jump into UDK and begin feeling comfortable using the most commonly used functions.

Specifically, we covered:

- ◆ How to download and install UDK
- ◆ How to launch the editor and the Autosave function
- ◆ How to navigate around the engine and how to use the short keys
- ◆ How to use BSP brushes and static meshes
- ◆ How to use the add and subtract operations used in BSP brushes
- ◆ How to scale and grid snap in UDK
- ◆ How to use different viewport options to maximize real time

Now that we've learned about the basics of navigating around the engine and using UDK's main features, we're ready to start creating our first map, which is the topic of the next chapter.

2
Hello UDK

UDK basics covers the most essential tools and functions you need to know to get started with UDK. You'll be able to quickly jump into UDK and begin feeling comfortable using the most commonly used functions.

In this chapter, we will learn the following:

- Setup, where to save the file, what to name it
- The builder brush and our first cube
- Geometry editing tool
- Building our first room
- Placing lights and a player start
- Creating a hallway and a second room
- Applying materials to CSG surfaces
- Test map and add bots

This is where the fun really starts. We will begin the first stages of creating our map by creating a small room, and then move onto adding features like lighting, materials, textures, and static meshes. This will be followed by adding a player start and testing our map with bots.

Your first map

You will build your first level using the unreal in-editor modeling system, **Constructive Solid Geometry (CSG)**, also referred to as BSP.

Time for action – setup, where to save the file, what to name it

1. Go to **File | New**, a window will pop up asking what geometry style you want, select **Additive**. Not only is it more appropriate for most level designs, but also I've seen some weird bugs with **Subtractive** mode in UDK.

2. Before we begin working, let's pick a name and save our file. For the purposes of this test, we'll use DM-CSGTest01.udk. Unreal figures out what game type you're making based on the map name. So by choosing DM-, we'll get a **Deathmatch** map, and all of the associated gameplay that comes with it as default lead-out. Go to **File | Save**. Unreal works best if you put your map in a specific folder, which you may have to create as follows:

   C:\UDK\UDK-VersionRelease\UDKGame\Content\Maps and name it DM-CSGTest01.udk.

3. Let's also do some viewport configuration to make editing easier. Click on **View | Viewport Configuration | 1x2 Split**. This will put your perspective view on the left and your top, and side 2D views on the right.

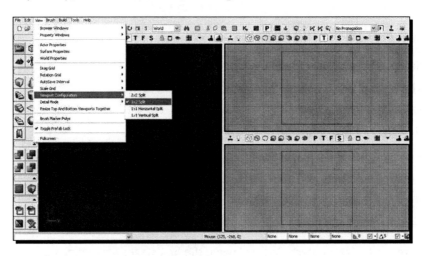

4. Click on **Unlit** mode in your perspective view. Since we're building a level from scratch, there won't be any lights yet, so we need to be in **Unlit** mode to see what we're doing.

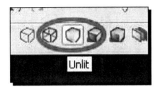

What just happened?

So we know how to set up our first level and how to select the addictive tool for our first attempt at designing our map. We know that it works best to save our level in the folder provided by UDK, and not set up our own to confuse things. We also know how to arrange and layout our viewport options. Finally, we know how to select the **Unlit** icon because we are creating our first map and there won't be any lighting just yet.

Why CSG?

We're going to use CSG geometry to rough out our level. It's the in-editor 3D modeling tool. While you could rough out the level in a 3D application such as Maya, Max, or even AutoCad, CSG gives you an incredibly fast turnaround when you begin working out the gameplay of your level. It's much easier than going back-and-forth between the different software packages.

That said, CSG isn't good for anything very detailed. It's expensive, it's hard to work with, and is prone to errors if the geometry gets too complicated. For this reason, it's great for prototyping since you don't want to add much detail in the early stages. It's also suitable for some simple geometry in the final level, as you can see in some of the epic's maps.

Time for action – the builder brush and our first cube

At the center of your empty level is a red wireframe cube. This is the builder brush. Think of it as a rubber stamp. Whatever shape and size it is, that's the shape and size of the geometry that you're going to stamp down.

1. Select the builder brush, then click on the **CSG : Add** button.

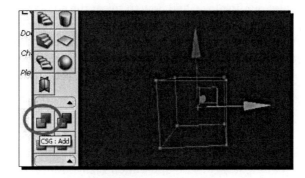

2. This stamps a cube down into the world, as shown in the following screenshot:

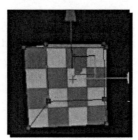

3. If you move the builder brush out of the way, you see that the cube stays in the 2D views. It appears as a blue wireframe box.

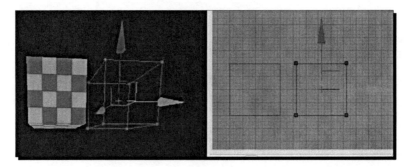

4. Now select the blue additive brush in one of the 2D views and move it to the side.

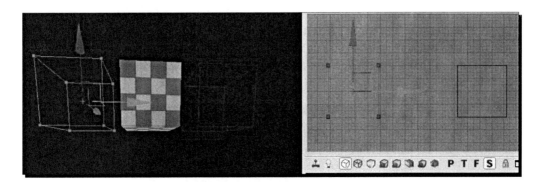

5. The checkerboard cube didn't move with it. When you modify existing the CSG, unreal requires you to **rebuild** for a simple cube move, which is pretty fast. But when you've got a whole level roughed-out in CSG, you wouldn't want unreal to pause and re-calculate all the time. Click on **Build Geometry for Current Level**, towards the top-right of the screen. You'll get some warnings, which are no big deal—that we'll discuss later—but the cube appears where it should appear.

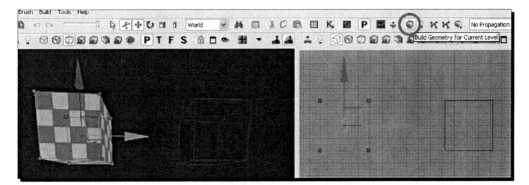

Subtractive

So say you wanted to create a room. You could place six additive cubes making up the walls, floor, and ceiling, but there's a better way to do it. In addition to additive, unreal has subtractive, and it does just what you'd think—it carves a hole in additive. Select the builder brush, move it so that it's partially intersecting with your additive brush, and click **CSG : Subtract**.

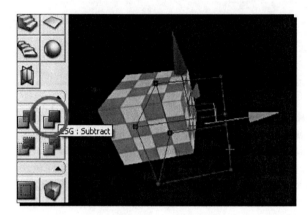

If you move the builder brush out of the way, you'll see that there's now a chunk taken out of your cube, and there's a yellow subtractive cube in the 2D view.

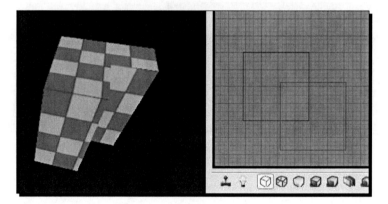

Try moving the subtractive brush around. You will again need to rebuild geometry in order for the changes to update in the 3D view.

Also, you can clone your additive or subtractive brushes by copying-and-pasting them (*ctrl+c*, *ctrl+v*), or by *alt*+dragging one of the movement handles. Play around a little more, intersect some more shapes, and rebuild. Get a feeling for the tools.

Brush Order

You may notice that sometimes a subtractive brush cuts into one additive brush, but not another.

This is because brushes are order dependent, they're like a set of commands such as `Build this`, `Now cut into it`, `Now build on top of that`, which are shown in the following screenshot:

If we want the subtractive brush to cut into both the additive brushes, we can make it the last command in the list. Select the subtractive brush, right-click on it, and select **Order | To Last**.

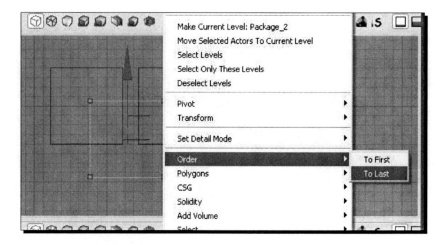

Now the brushes are in the order we want.

And if we rebuild geometry, we get the results we want.

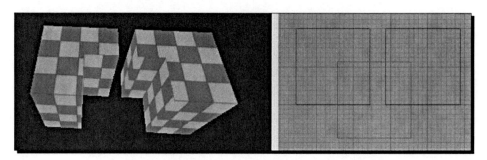

And yes, you could have also selected the #3 additive brushes and clicked on **Order | To First**, to get the same result.

What just happened?

So we know how to use the builder brush tool to create our first cube. Let's go ahead and look at the geometry editing mode tool.

Time for action – geometry editing tool

Let's face it; it would be tough to build a level solely out of cubes. Let's look at some more advanced geometry editing. But first, save your work, create a new file, and save it as DM-CSGTest02.udk.

1. Create a new additive brush, then click on the **Geometry Mode** button at the top-left corner of the window. This opens up the **Geometry Tools** dialog box. You can close it again by clicking on the button to the left, **Camera Mode**.

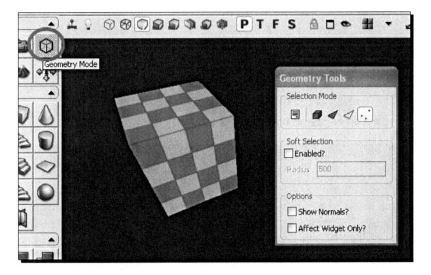

2. Working with edges is the easiest way to get started, so click on the **Edge** button, and select your additive cube.

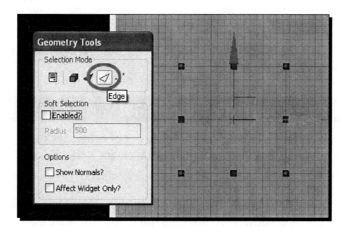

3. Make sure you're in the **World** mode (not **Local**).

4. Then select an edge and try moving it around.

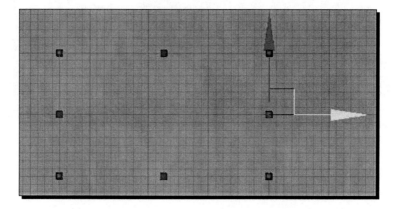

5. Now our cube is an elongated rectangular box. Don't forget to rebuild geometry.

6. You'll notice that when you selected the edge in the 2D view, it actually selected two edges in the 3D view—in my case, the top and bottom. This is really handy and what you want most of the time. But you can also make a ramp shape by selecting only one of the edges in the 3D view and then moving it.

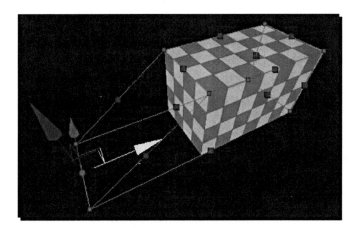

7. Editing vertices is also pretty powerful. Switch back to **Vertex** mode.

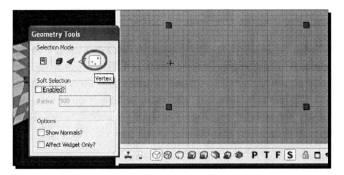

8. You can select any vertex and move it around. You can also *ctrl*+click to select multiple vertices, or *ctrl+alt*+click+drag to make a selection box.

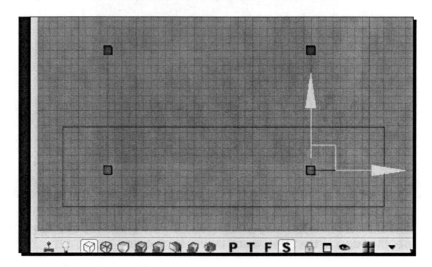

 ctrl+alt+drag works for anything in unreal, not just geometry editing. You can *ctrl+alt*+right click+drag to deselect.

Play with your shape some more and get a sense for how to do some serious geometry editing.

What just happened?

We know how to use the CSG tool to map out a rough outline of our first room. So let's begin with building our first room.

Time for action – building our first room

Time to create our first room, something we can actually run around in. Save your work, create a new file, and save it as DM-CSGTest03.udk.

We want our room to be big enough for the player to run around in. The builder brush is 256x256x256 by default, and the player is 88 units tall. That's going to feel a little cramped, so let's make our cube more like 1024x1024x512 units tall. What we're going to do is create an additive cube which is the size we want, and then hollow it out by using a slightly smaller subtractive cube. Select the builder brush and make sure you're in the **Geometry** mode. Yes, the geometry editing tools work on the builder brush too.

Also, resize your grid to 32 units either by using the controls in the bottom-right corner of the screen or the bracket [ ] keys. It's important to build on the grid so that we have an easier time-judging size, and so that when we expand our level later, everything lines up nicely. This is also why we're using the **Geometry tools** to resize the brush instead of non-uniformly scaling it. Your setup should look like the following screenshot:

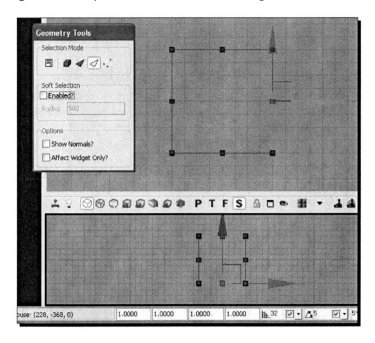

So we're going to grab the builder brush's edges and move them around until the brush is big enough, but how do we tell how big it is? There's nothing that tells us the cube's size directly. We can use the measure tool to drag in a 2D view and measure distances. Just click-and-drag with the middle mouse button.

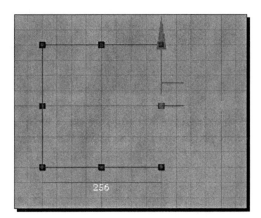

Drag the builder brush's edges until it's of the right size. Make sure that you also check the side view, and make the brush 512 units tall.

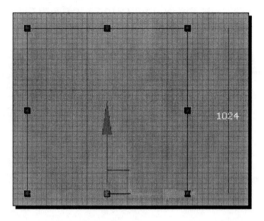

Click **CSG : Add**, and your box will appear in the 3D view.

 The checkerboard on the surface, tiles a lot more on a bigger cube.

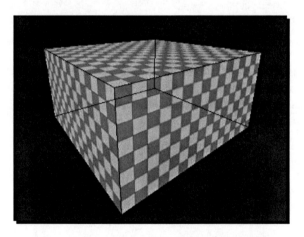

Now resize your builder brush in both the top and side views to fit just inside of the additive brush and hit **CSG : Subtract**. If you fly the camera inside the cube you can see that it's hollow.

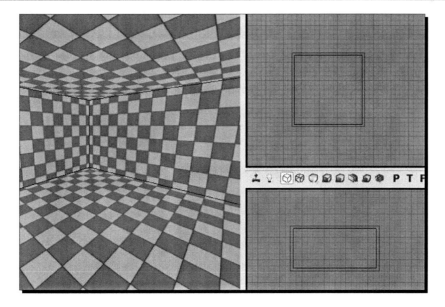

We're almost ready to play, but we need some default lighting and we need to tell unreal where the player is going to spawn.

What just happened?

We know how to create our first room. Let's go ahead and add some light to our room.

Have a go hero – second floor

So you have a basic room, why not try to create another room? See if you can create another room on top of the one you just created, subtract a hole in the room, and add a staircase or maybe a elevator which takes you into the second room.

Time for action – placing lights and a player start

In this section, we'll be placing actors, so we'll be mostly working in the 3D view. Close the **Geometry tools** window, click on the **Camera Mode** button, and save your work. First we'll place a light. It is easy—right-click on the ground, then click on **Add Actor | Add Light (Point)**.

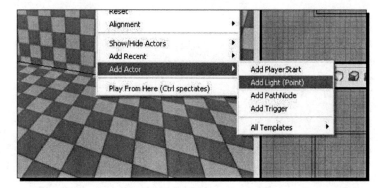

The light should appear where you clicked. Go to **Lit** mode, and you'll see your room appear with lighting now, though it looks a little strange, since the light is right on the floor.

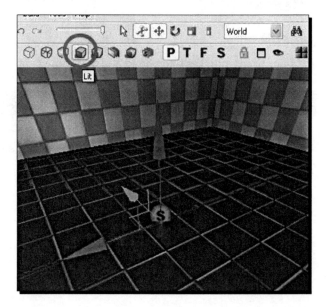

Move the light up from the floor so it's in the middle of the room. You can also increase or decrease the light's radius using the **Scale** tool. Give it a try.

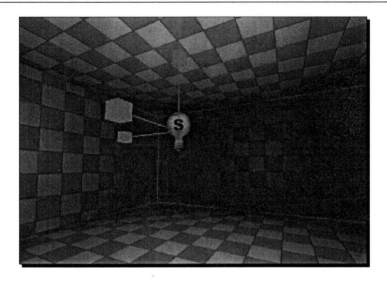

The last thing we need to do before we run is to **Bake Lighting**. Right now the light is calculated dynamically, which is expensive and unnecessary. If we bake it, it calculates texture maps for any light and shadows in the scene, which is much cheaper. Click on the **Build Lighting** tool that is right next to **Build Geometry**. The default settings in the **Options** window are fine, so hit **OK**.

Baking should go pretty fast since this is a really simple scene. But for a finished level, it can take up to an hour depending on your machine, the size of the level, and the complexity of the lighting, of course. One last thing before we can play, Create a **Player Start**—which is the same as adding a light. Right-click on the floor, then click **Add Actor | Add PlayerStart**. The player start should appear at a proper height off the ground.

Save your work. To run the level, click on the **Play in Editor** button in the top-right corner of the window, it looks like a little joystick.

What just happened?

So we have added some light to our room. Let's now go ahead and create a hallway along with a second room.

Have a go hero – advanced lighting

We know a little bit about lighting up our room. Why not try to add more lights to your room, give your room some color by playing around with the light properties, and strengthen or weaken the light to suit the atmosphere of your room.

Time for action – creating a hallway and a second room

At this point, you should be able to create a second room and a hallway without any more guidance, but I'll take this opportunity to show a few more tricks. Save your work, and then save it as a new file, DM-CSGTest04.udk.

We'll create the second room first, and then the hallway.

Instead of building the second room from scratch, let's select the first room and everything in it, and then clone it over. In one of the 2D views, *ctrl+alt*+drag a selection box around the entire room. We want the player start and the light too, which will be useful later.

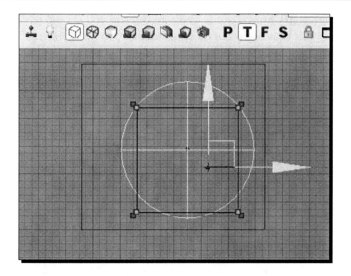

Then *alt*+drag on the **Move** tool to copy the room over to the right side.

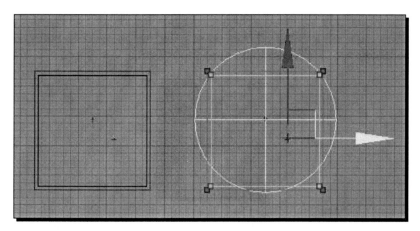

Press the **Rebuild Geometry** button, go to **Unlit** mode, and you should see both rooms in your 3D view. Remember that there are no lights outside, so the outer surfaces will show up black.

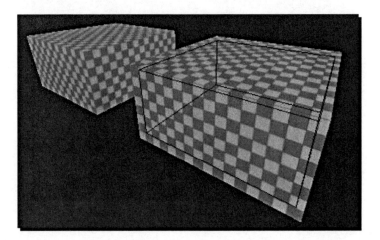

Time to create the hallway. We could clone a room again and shrink it down using the geometry editor tools, but let's build it from scratch. Clicking on the **Cube** button on the left will reset the builder brush to the default 256x256x256 cube.

But if you right-click on it, you get a dialog box where you can type in how big you want the cube to be. Measure how far apart your rooms are, and fill that into the properties. Mine were 512 units apart in the Y-dimension. 256 is fine for the corridor's width and height (X and Z).

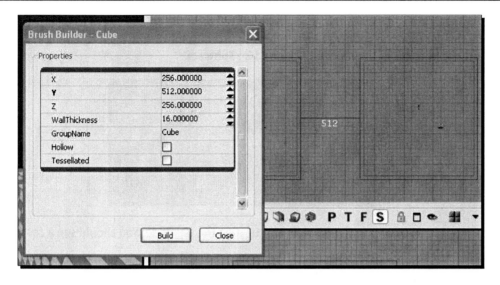

Click on **Build**, place the builder brush between your rooms, and click on **CSG : Add**.

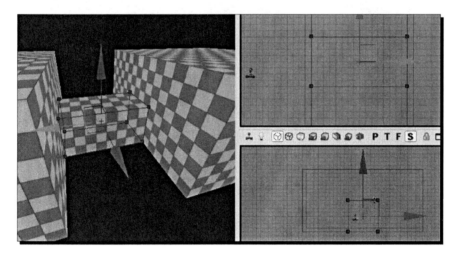

Now, like with the rooms, use the geometry tools to resize the builder brush to be just slightly smaller than the additive brush. Most importantly, make sure it's long enough to connect the interiors of the rooms. Click on **CSG : Subtract**.

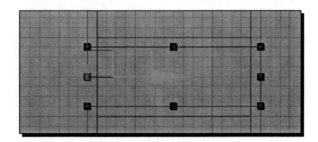

Go back inside the rooms in the 3D view and turn on the **Lit** mode. You should see a corridor connecting your rooms.

Add some extra lights to the hallway. Instead of going through all that right-click nonsense, you can hold the *l* key (*l* for **light**) and click on the floor. Rebuild lighting, save your work, and test your level.

What just happened?

We now have a hallway and a second room, but it looks a little bland. Let's see if we can add some atmosphere and color to our rooms by applying some materials to the surfaces.

Time for action – applying materials to CSG surfaces

It's time to get rid of that grey checkerboard pattern covering the walls and floor. You can apply either a material or a material instance to a surface. We'll discuss the differences later. Both types of materials show up in the generic browser with a green border.

MI_LT_Doors_SM_Door01
Parent: M_Shader_Simple

Let's find a material that we can apply to our CSG surfaces. Open the generic browser, and in the filter list, check **Material** and **Material Instance Constant**. If you have anything else checked, like **Static Mesh**, uncheck it.

Click on some packages. Any of them starting with HU_ contain human environment assets, which is a good start. You'll see that a few materials show up, but not many. This is because the packages haven't been fully loaded yet.

Select a package, right-click on it, and select **Fully Load**. You can select multiple packages at the same time by *ctrl+*clicking on their names, or by *shift+*clicking to select a block. Select all of the HU_ packages now, and fully load them. You'll have a lot more materials to choose from. Applying a material to a surface is really easy. Select the surface (click on it in the 3D view), then click on a material in the generic browser. The material will appear. Try it now.

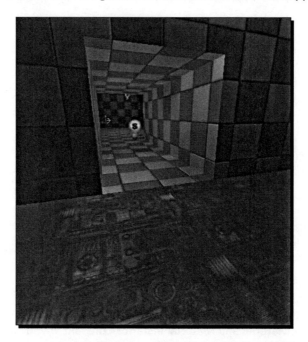

One thing to watch out for is that some materials have transparent parts.

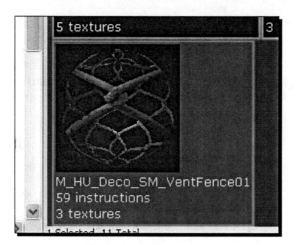

Now, you could select the surfaces in your level one-by-one and apply materials, but there are some tools for selecting multiple surfaces at once. First, you can select multiple surfaces at once by holding the *ctrl* key and clicking on them one-by-one. Try that now. You can also *ctrl*+click a selected face to unselect it. There are also a bunch of options under the right-click menu.

I won't go into the details, but try a few of these options and see what they do. You might want to start with **Matching Texture**, that'll select all checkerboard surfaces. You could also try **Matching Brush** to select the entire room, or **Adjacent Walls** to select all the connected walls.

Take a few minutes now and replace all checkerboard surfaces in your level with appropriate-looking floors, walls, and ceilings.

Surface Properties

Now let's look at how to change the alignment, rotation, or scale of your material. Select a face and go to **View | Surface Properties** (or hit *F5*).

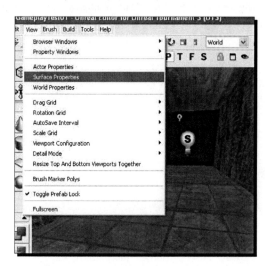

The best way to learn the tool is to try it out for yourself.

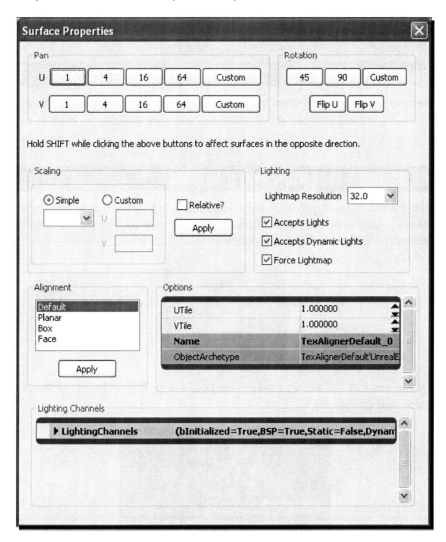

Panning and rotating are easy; just click the button you want and the material updates on the surface. You can *shift*+click on a button to move or rotate in the opposite direction. Changing the scale is nearly as easy, but once you select a scale option, you need to press the **Apply** button just to the right of the scale. The default scale is 1, and larger numbers mean that the material will cover a larger area. The other things you can control on this menu are the surface's lighting properties, but we'll discuss that in detail when we talk about lighting.

What just happened?

So our map has a little character to it. Let's now test our map, add some bots, and get an idea of what our map will play like.

Have a go hero – adding more elements to your level

So we know how to add a player start, but what else can we add to our level? Open up the content browser and see if you can add weapons, power ups, and special abilities to your map.

Time for action – test map and add bots

I'll cover this in much more depth later, but it would be fun at this point to add some bots to the level. Make sure your map name starts with DM- and save your work. In the editor, click the **Build All** button to the right of **Build Lighting**.

Save your game and run it. Open up the console by pressing *Tab*, and type addbots 1. A bot should appear, and you can kill it.

To add more bots, add more player start nodes, rebuild all, run the level, and type addbots [number] in the console. Have fun with it. Try adding some additional rooms, and make a more interesting layout. See if you can make ramps to rooms at different heights, or raised platforms inside the room.

What just happened?

So we have now tested our map with bots and have an idea of what our map will play like with these two rooms and a hallway.

Have a go hero – content browser

So we know how to add a player start, but what else can we add to our level. Open up the content browser and see if you can add weapons, power ups, and special abilities to your map.

Have a go hero – bot navigation

We can add bots to our level by using the console bar, but as the bots have no navigation around your map, why not try to add bot pathing? This is reasonably simple but can get tricky, so make sure that you have alot of time and patience to get it right.

Pop quiz

What viewport configuration did we use when setting up our map?

1. 2x2 Split
2. 2x1 Split
3. 1x1 Horizontal Split
4. 1x1 Vertical Split

Summary

We learned a lot in this chapter.

Specifically, we covered:

- How to set up our level and configure viewport options and unlit settings
- How to build a basic room
- How to add light to our basic room
- How to add player starts to our level
- How to create surfaces in our room
- How to apply a material to a surface
- Finally, how to test our level and add bots

We know how to create a basic room and add characteristics such as light and materials to surfaces, we also know how to test our map with bots. We're now ready to look further into lighting and how to get the most out of it.

3
Applying Lighting Effects

This section covers lighting in UDK. I will be looking at the different types of lighting used in developing and designing an environment in UDK, and how light maps are used on CSG surfaces and static meshes to reflect the light of objects.

In this chapter, we will learn:

◆ Different types of lighting

◆ Light maps

◆ Adjusting lightmaps on CSG surfaces

◆ Lightmaps on static meshes

Let's crack on!

To get you started, here are some of the **roles** that lighting can fill in your scene.

Directional lights

◆ **The sun**

◆ **Ambient sky light:** Try placing multiple lights, all with a low brightness and a bluish color, facing downward in the four cardinal directions

Point lights

- ◆ **Area lights**: Dim, filling a corridor with bounce light
- ◆ **Highlights**: Small radius, probably near the spotlight meshes
- ◆ **Bounce lights**: If a bright light hits the floor, it will bounce up and light-up the walls and ceiling a little too

Spotlights

- ◆ **Spotlights**: A cone of light projecting from a spotlight mesh
- ◆ **Fill lights**: Blue light pouring in between the arches, hitting mostly the floor
- ◆ **Bounce lights**: Similar to point lights, but a little more control

Skylights

- ◆ You may want to add some additional ambient light to the scene using a skylight.

Time for action – different types of light

So let's start going into more detail with the different types of lighting used in UDK, starting with point lights.

Point lights

1. Placing a point light is easy—right-click on a surface and choose **Add Actor | Add Light (Point)** or just hold down the *l* key (for **light**) and click on a surface. A point light will appear. Go into **Lit** mode, press *F4* to bring up the light's properties, and then open up the **Light** category and the **LightComponent** subcategory.

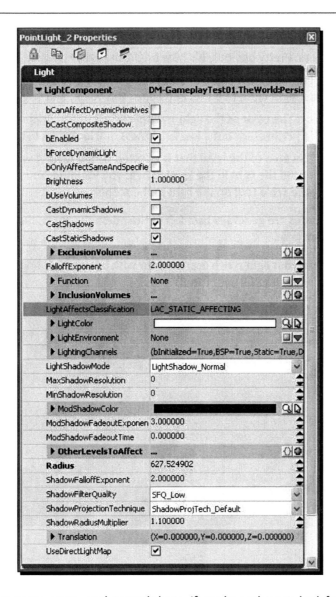

There are some pretty cool controls here, if you know how to look for them. For instance, if you want to change the brightness of the light, you can type in a new number in place of **1.000000**. Or, if you hold the mouse between the two black arrows on the right, you'll see it change to a double-arrow icon. Click-and-drag up and down and you'll change the brightness dynamically.

2. Next, to the **LightColor** field, you can click the magnifying glass to bring up a color palette display. You can also click on the mouse pointer icon to get a color picker, click in the scene to sample the surface's color. Try both of those now.

3. I'll list the most important properties here. Be sure to try each one on your own.

- ◆ **Brightness**: Pretty obvious, it's how bright the light appears.
- ◆ **FalloffExponent**: How sharp or soft the light's fall off appears within its radius. Move your light close to a wall and adjust this value, and you'll see how it works.
- ◆ **LightColor**: The color of the light multiplies against the brightness setting. So if you pick a bright color but a low brightness, it'll look dark in the scene.
- ◆ **Radius**: The area of the level that is affected by the light. A wireframe sphere is drawn around the light in the level to help you visualize. You can also adjust this by using the **scale** tool on the light in the scene.

Other properties are generally best left at their default values, though we'll discuss some of them later.

4. For now, make your light a rich orange color with a fairly high brightness and a radius large enough to fill your room.

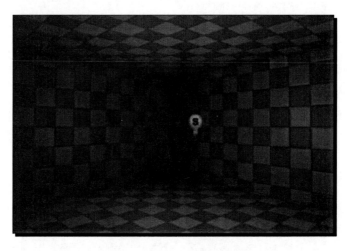

Spotlights

Placing a spotlight is a little harder than placing a point light—they can be found under the **Actor Classes** browser.

1. So open your generic browser and go to the **Actor Classes** tab. Open up the **Light** category and select **Spot Light**. You'll notice two subcategories, **SpotLightMovable** and **SpotLightToggleable**. These are mainly used in animation sequences or hooked up to gameplay, so ignore them for now.

2. Right-click in your scene and select **Add SpotLightHere**. A white spotlight appears, pointing down. Move it so that it's casting a circle of light on the ground.

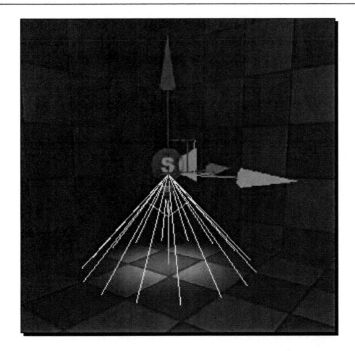

3. Spotlights have all of the same important properties as point lights (color, brightness, radius, and falloff), but they have a few additional properties as well. Make sure your spotlight is selected and opens up its properties. Look for two new properties.

- ◆ **OuterConeAngle**: How wide of an angle the cone covers.

- ◆ **InnerConeAngle**: Controls the hotspot in the middle of the cone. If it's 0, it'll cast a very soft circle of light. If this is the same radius as the OuterConeAngle, the spotlight will cast a hard-edged circle of light, but you may lose detail when you bake lighting.

4. You can rotate a spotlight using the standard rotation tool in the editor. You can also control it in first-person mode (like holding a flashlight) by clicking on **Lock Selected Actors to the Camera** on top of your perspective viewport.

5. Update your spotlight's cone angle to cover a wider area, and point it at a wall.

Directional lights

As I mentioned earlier, a directional light is like the sun. So what's going to happen if I place one in this room? After all, there are no windows.

1. Place a directional light now in the same way you paced a spot light—select it under the **Actor Classes** browser.

   It doesn't really seem to be affecting the scene, except for a weird shimmering effect on the walls. And if you bake lighting or rotate the light, the shimmering goes away.

2. Even though the icon for the light is inside the room, the light is only affecting the outside of the level. Much like the sun, the walls of the rooms are casting a shadow on the interior of the rooms. So a directional light is really only useful in an outdoor scene. And even then, you have to turn off **Cast Shadows** on any SkyDome object you've placed. Rotate the light slightly so that it's not facing straight down.

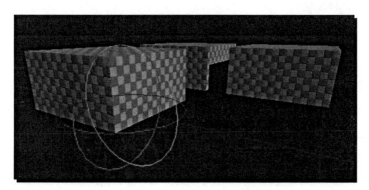

3. Rotating a directional light works the same way as rotating a spot light, but instead of having a light cone to indicate the direction, you've got a little blue arrow.

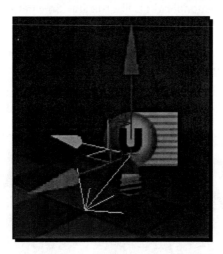

Skylights

Skylights are a good way to add a small amount of ambient light to your level. They're also great during the prototyping phase since they cast light on everything in the scene and they don't slow down much of your frame rate. Their big disadvantage is that they don't cast shadows, so even interiors will receive light from a skylight.

1. Let's place one now (same method as the other light types)

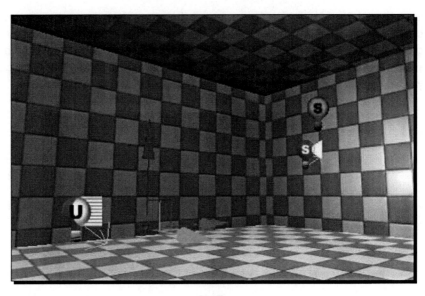

2. Immediately the scene gets much brighter except for the ceiling, which is unaffected. The light is brightening up every surface based on the angle relative to **up**. So the floor gets a lot of light, walls get a medium amount of light, and the ceiling gets no light. We can adjust the brightness and color of this light, and in fact we can add in **bounce** light that affects the ceiling as well. Open up the properties for your skylight now, and play with the settings. There are only two new ones you haven't seen yet.

   ◆ **LowerBrightness**: The brightness of the **under** light (default to 0)

   ◆ **LowerColor**: The color of the **under** light

   Adjust the skylight's properties so that the color from above is bright red, and the color from below is bright blue or vice-versa (with a bright enough LowerBrightness so that it's visible).

   Ok, that's pretty hideous, but notice how the red and the blue are combining to make a purple color on the walls. It should be especially obvious if you delete your point light.

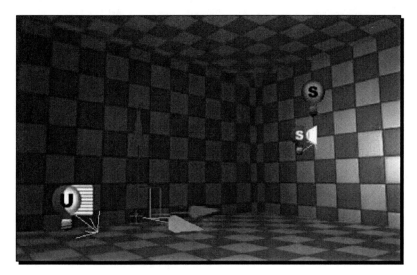

2. One last thing—the icon for that skylight is very small, and it's likely to get lost in a large level. In the properties, under the **Display** category, change the **DrawScale** to 10.000000. It's much easier to find now.

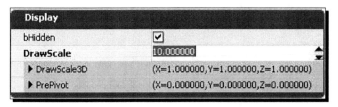

What just happened?

So we know about the different variations of lighting used in UDK. Point lights are used to light up a room, spotlights focus their light on a certain area of your map, and directional lighting is like a sun and is used to light up large parts of your map. Skylights focus more on ambient lighting than world lighting. Let's look into lighting up a room with these different variations of lighting.

Time for action – lightmaps

1. When you bake lighting on your scene, the lighting data gets stored into one or more images called lightmaps. Open up an existing scene that's a simple CSG room with a light in it, as shown in the following screenshot:

2. Save your scene (call it DM-LightmapTest.udk) and bake lighting. Now look in your generic browser, and you'll see a package named DM-LightmapTest. If you select it, you'll see four texture images in it. These are the lightmaps that got baked for your cube. I won't go into why there are four of them—the reasons are technical and they won't affect your work. If you create a bigger level, the lightmaps will be bigger because they cover more surface area.

3. Now switch back to the main editor window and click the **Lighting Only** button in your perspective viewport. The checkerboard goes away and you're left with just the lighting. But notice that it's a little blotchy. This is because there's not a lot of detail in the lightmap. After all, those images in the generic browser were pretty small.

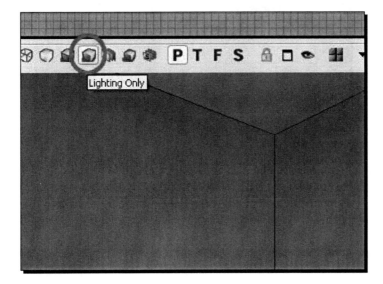

4. Ok, maybe it's not that obvious. It'll be much clearer if we put a static mesh in the world that casts a shadow on the wall. In the `HU_Deco3` package, there's a fire hydrant prop (named `S_HU_Deco_SM_FireHydrant01`). Place that in the world between your light and the wall. It's a pretty small prop, so scale it larger, at least `4 x` `sizes`.

If you bake lighting, you'll see a big blurry shadow on the wall. That's the effect of having a low-detailed lightmap.

What just happened?

So we know what lightmaps are and how they can be assigned to static meshes to create a blurry shadow effect when light is beamed of the static mesh, but it doesn't look very realistic. So let's go ahead and look at adjusting the lightmap by going into the surface properties of the mesh.

Time for action – adjusting lightmaps on CSG surfaces

1. Go back into **Lit** mode and select the wall that has the blurry shadow on it. Open up the **Surface Properties** window by going to **View | Surface Properties** or by hitting *F5*.

2. We've covered most of these settings in an earlier tutorial, but let's look at the **Lighting** section, specifically the **Lightmap Resolution** parameter.

3. A setting of 32.0 means that there'll be one lightmap pixel every 32 units. If we want more detail (and we do!), we can make that number smaller. Set it to 4 and bake again. You'll notice that the bake takes much longer, but you've got a much more obvious shadow from the fire hydrant. If you try setting the resolution to 1, it may take over a minute to bake, but the results look even better.

4. Go back to the generic browser and find your map. You'll notice that some new lightmap textures have been created (and the old ones may still be hanging around too—UDK will clean those up later). If you look closely at your lightmap, you can see one big square with a shadow of the fire hydrant on it, and five tiny blurry squares. That adds up to the six sides of your room.

5. And that's about it. If you need more detail, set the **Lightmap Resolution** to a lower value, but keep in mind your bake times will suffer.

What just happened?

So we know if we adjust lightmaps on CSG surfaces using the surface properties, specifically changing the **Lightmap Resolution** settings, we can adjust shadows to make them look more realistic when light hits the mesh. The next stage would be to shine the light of static meshes.

Have a go hero – reduce lightmap resolution on surfaces

If you are up for a challenge, try to optimize BSP surfaces. Set the resolution to 65536, and uncheck **Accepts Lights**, **Accepts Dynamic Lights**, and **Force Lightmap**. Also apply the material RemoveSurfaceMaterial from the EngineMaterials package.

Time for action – lightmaps on static meshes

Baking lighting on static meshes is a little more versatile than on CSG geo. By default, all static meshes use vertex lighting—instead of baking into an image, light values get baked into the vertices that make up the geometry, and lighting is blended across the surface.

1. In my map, there's a kind of a weird hard shadow near the top of the fire hydrant.

2. If I overlay the wireframe on the image (Photo-shopped for clarity), you can see that the shadow falls right along one of the mesh's edges. That's effectively the result you get from vertex lighting.

3. But lots of meshes in UDK are set up so that you can put a lightmap on them too, and this fire hydrant is one of them. Open up the mesh in the generic browser and look at the **LightMapCoordinateIndex** value. If it's **1**, then the mesh is probably set up for lightmaps, otherwise it probably isn't.

So how do we actually turn on the lightmap?

4. Close the **Static Mesh Editor**, select the fire hydrant in the scene, and open up its properties (hit *F4*). Open up **StaticMeshActor**, **StaticMeshComponent**, scroll all the way to the bottom, and open the **StaticMeshComponent** subcategory.

5. Right now, **bOverrideLightMapResolution** is checked, and
OverriddenLightMapResolution is set to **0**. The **0** means it's using vertex lighting.

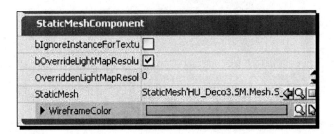

6. On CSG surfaces, a smaller number meant more detail. This is because the number
specifies how far apart lightmap pixels will be calculated. On a static mesh, you
control the size of the lightmap image directly. If you type 4, it'll calculate a 4x4
image to paint the lighting onto, which definitely isn't enough detail. You'd get
better results with vertex lighting.

Change the number to 64 and also bake lighting. You'll see that the hard lines are
gone, and the lighting generally looks better. You can go higher to get even more
precise results, but again, baking will start to take a lot longer and for an object this
small, it's probably not necessary.

7. If you open up the generic browser again and look at your map, you can see that the
lightmap has updated again. It's got the six sides from the room, plus an additional
patch of scattered detail. This is the lightmap for your fire hydrant:

What just happened?

So we know that vertex lighting comes as standard when using lightmaps to direct light of static meshes, but the shadow can leave odd shapes. By using something called bake lighting, we can adjust the shadow surface properties, so that it completely covers the static mesh when light hits it, making it far more realistic. The most important thing when being a level-designer is attention to detail.

Have a go hero – creating lightmaps for custom static meshes

If you create your own environment props, you may want to add lightmaps to them. The best way to do this is to create the UVs in your 3D package (Max or Maya), but we can also auto-generate lightmap UVs inside unreal. Let's see how to do this. Create a sphere in your 3D package and import it. Double-click the mesh to open-up the **Static Mesh Editor**. Go to **View | UV Overlay**, and you'll see the default set of UVs. To create the second UV set, go to **Mesh | Generate Unique UVs**. Change the **UV Channel...** parameter to **1** and hit **OK**. Now, change the **LightMapCoordinateIndex** to **1**, and you'll see the result of the auto-UV generation.

Pop quiz

What are the four different types of lighting used in UDK?

Summary

We learned a lot in this chapter about:

- The different types of lighting used when designing in UDK
- What lightmaps are and how to apply them
- How to adjust lightmaps on CSG surfaces
- Lightmaps on static meshes

So what have we learnt? We have learnt about the different types of lighting used in UDK. We know the basics of light mapping and how we can apply them to CSG surfaces and static meshes. In the next chapter, we will be looking at the different particle effects used to bring depth and character to our level.

4
Battling the Elements

This is a basic chapter on how the effects work using Unreal Engine 3's particle editor (cascade). It will quickly walk you through the interface of the editor and explain how a basic smoke particle, water, height, and fog can be set up.

In this chapter, we will cover the following topics:

- The basics
- Add a new particle emitter
- The smoke example
- Adding height fog
- Creating the surface
- Water volumes
- Underwater

Let's Go!

To start with, we are going to look into the basics of cascade particles. The particle system in UDK is drastically different to its original UE2 variant. Particles now have a brand-new and extensive particle editor, and are saved as assets in a package, instead of actors in a level or a U file.

The ability to save a particle as an asset in a package is great, since all levels can now refer to the same particle, and if the particle has to be adjusted, it will only have to be done once.

The new particle system is module-based. You add blocks of **stuff**, if you want to extend a particle. Each module contains new features and properties. We will get back to that a bit later.

Time for action – the basics

1. The cascade **Particle Editor** can be accessed only through an already existing particle. Thus, if you want to open the editor, you should either double-click an existing particle in the generic browser or simply create a brand new one.

2. To create a brand new particle, open the generic browser, right-click in some empty space, and choose **New Particle System**.

3. If all is right, the cascade **Particle Editor** will open automatically once the new particle has been created. Particles have a yellow edge in the generic browser. If you cannot see it, it might be hidden. Enable the **Particle Systems** in the top-left of the generic browser to show it, or simply enable the option **Show All Resource Types**.

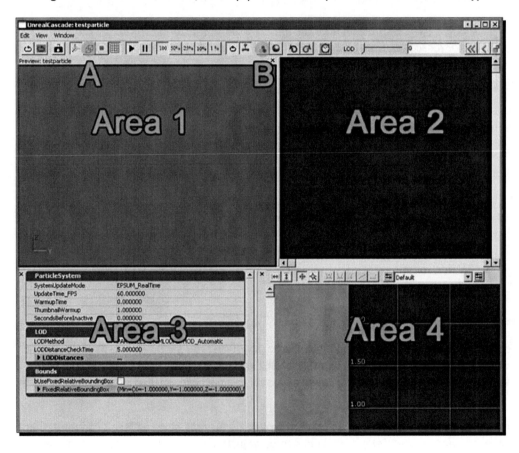

- ❑ **Area 1**: This is the **preview** window and will preview the particle effect.

- ❑ **Area 2**: This is the **list** of different particle emitters and all of the modules that each emitter contains. A **Particle System** can contain multiple particle emitters. It is possible to have a water-drip effect and a water-splash effect in the same **Particle System**, much like what was possible in UE3. Right now this space is still black because there are no particle emitters yet.

- ❑ **Area 3**: This is the **property section**, and will display the properties of whichever emitter or module is selected.

- ❑ **Area 4**: This is the **curve editor**, which is used to make smooth transitions from one value to another.

4. The top toolbar also has two buttons of interest. The wireframe button A and the background color button B. The reason why I mention those two buttons is because it can be very hard to see certain particles, (the smaller ones, especially), in the viewport, and it often appears as if there's nothing at all. Switching to a wireframe view might help to reveal where the particles are and how large they are. All other buttons are not too relevant right now.

Time for action – add a new particle emitter

1. Add a new **Particle Emitter** by right-clicking anywhere in **Area 2** and clicking on the only option given (**New ParticleSpriteEmitter**). You now have a very basic particle.

2. Now, you obviously want to modify the default set up. To do so, you can click on any of the modules, such as **Lifetime** or **Initial Size**. If you need more than the default settings, you can right-click anywhere in the column and you will get a list of additional modules that you can add.

What just happened?

So now we know what particle emitters are and that they are used for adding depth and character to our map. We also know how they can be created using the particle editor. So what's the next step? Let's go ahead and start by creating a smoke effect.

Time for action – the smoke example

Since an example can best explain it, we will go through all the steps required to make a basic smoke particle set up that spawns and rotates particles, fades in and out, and grows in size.

1. First of all, you need a cloud material. Create your own cloud texture or use mine. Right-click this image and save it somewhere. Preferably, convert it to BMP or TGA before you import it.

2. Add the texture to a **Material** and set it up as displayed in the following screenshot:

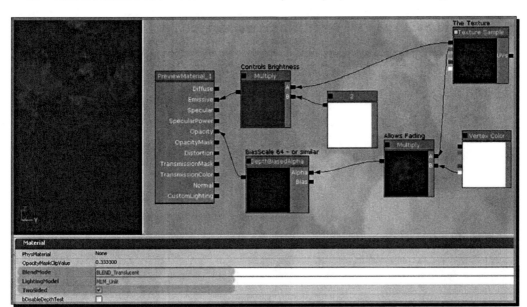

3. The **DepthBiasedAlpha** will make sure that it is a soft particle. When a particle sprite intersects with a piece of geometry, the **DepthBiasedAlpha** will fade-out the sprite along the edge.

4. The **Vertex Color** expression is really important. All materials that are used in particles must have a **Vertex Color** expression because it allows cascade to change the opacity and color of the particles. Without a **Vertex Color**, you cannot fade-out a particle, for example.

5. Once the material has been set up it can be applied to the **Particle System**. Be sure to have the material selected in the generic browser, then select the **Particle Emitter** in **Area 2** and assign the material to the marked spot.

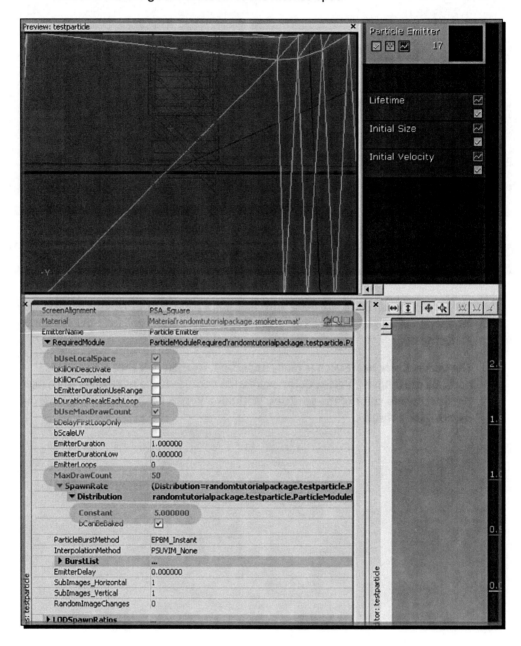

6. In newer versions of the engine, the properties displayed in the previous screenshot have moved to the sections **Spawn** and **Required** instead. Next, open the section **RequiredModule** right below the **Material** input field and modify the following properties:

   ❑ **bUseLocalSpace**: Enable **bUseLocalSpace**. This will enable the particle to move around more easily, and it adds the possibility of rotating it with the regular rotation tool.

   ❑ **bUseMaxDrawCount**: Enable **bUseMaxDrawCount**. This will cap the maximum number of particles at the **MaxDrawCount** number, instead of keep spawning particles that are dependent on the height of the **SpawnRate** number.

   ❑ **MaxDrawCount**: Set **MaxDrawCount** to 50. This will limit the maximum number of particle sprites.

   ❑ **SpawnRate Constant**: Set **SpawnRate Constant** to 5.000000. This controls the number of particles spawned every second.

7. Leave all other settings as the default settings for the time being.

 If the particle only shows up in wireframe view, don't panic. It may be normal behavior because of the **VertexColor** node in the **Material** editor, and will be resolved later.

8. Select the **Lifetime** module in **Area 2** so that its properties show up in **Area 3**. In that module, change **Max** to 3.0 and **Min** to 2.5. This controls the maximum time a particle lives before disappearing again. Click on the next module—which is **Initial Size**—and set **Max X**, **Y**, and **Z** to 256.0 each and **Min X**, **Y**, and **Z** to 224 each. This will give the particle a random size ranging between 224 and 256. Feel free to use any other kind of number too, of course, so that the difference in size is not big enough for you.

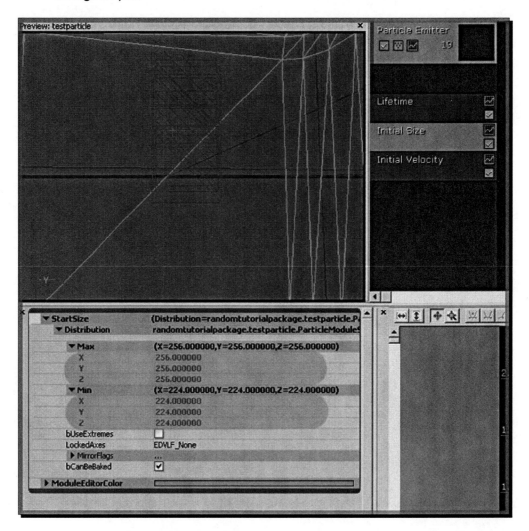

9. After that, select the module **Initial Velocity**, and set **Max X** and **Y** to 8 each, and **Z** to 160. Set **Min X** and **Y** to -8 each, and **Z** to 128.

Velocity controls the direction and speed. In this case, the smoke will rise with a speed between `128` and `160`, and will have a subtle random movement to either the left, right, front, or back.

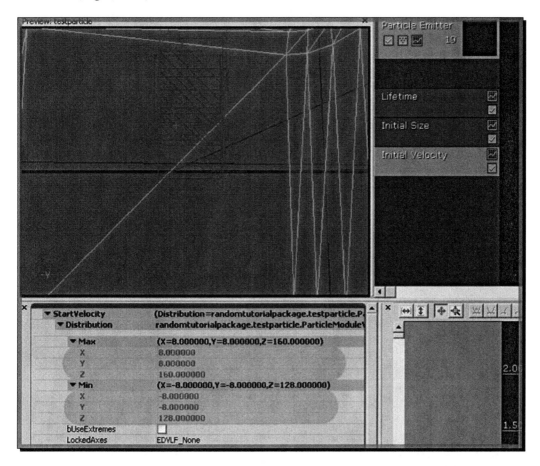

10. The next thing you want to do is give a random start location to the smoke, since you don't want all of the sprites to start exactly at the same location. The default modules do not allow you to set a random start location, so you will have to add a new module to the **Particle Emitter**.

Right-click in the column of the **Particle Emitter** in **Area 2**, and choose **Location | Initial Location**. Once added, click on it to get to its properties, change all **Max** numbers to 2.0 and all **Min** numbers to -2. This gives you a four unit width box in any direction, and thus a maximum of four units offset for a particle.

 If you click the red crossed box on the module, the viewport will show a wireframe box to indicate the spawning area.

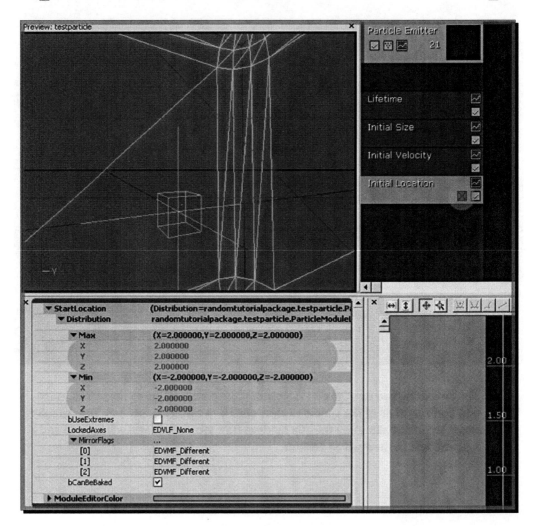

11. Now there are two more things that you want to do before the smoke particle is done: Fade out and make it grow. Both actions are performed by using the curve editor.

12. Let's tackle the fading first. Right-click the particle emitter column and add a new module: **Color | ColorOverLife**. If your particle didn't show up in a non-wireframe view at first, it probably will do so now.

13. To add the **ColorOverLife** module to the curve editor and finally gain some functionality for it, click the little button on the module. Curves can be hidden by clicking on the little yellow square in the left column of the curve editor. Do so for the **ColorOverLife** curve, since you don't need this at all right now, but it will be available when working with the alpha curve.

14. Now, you may notice that you either can't see the alpha curve or that you can't add extra control points to it. The reason for this is because the **AlphaOverLife** curve is always wrongly configured by default, it is configured as a constant simple number, and you obviously don't want a simple number, but a whole curve to control it.

15. Expand **AlphaOverLife** in the properties section to the left and click on **Distribution** until you get a blue triangle button on the right of it. Click that triangle and choose **DistributionFloatConstantCurve**.

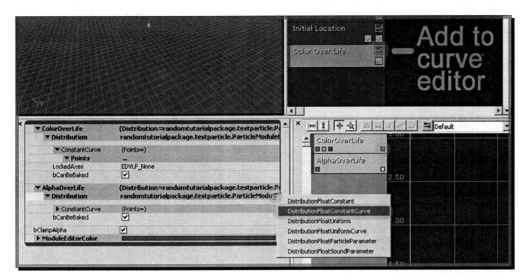

16. Left-clicking and dragging makes you pan through the curve editor view, the mouse wheel zooms in and out. If all is right, you will see a flat purple (could have another color too) line in it. This is the **AlphaOverLife** curve. The horizontal numbers are the **time**, and the vertical ones are the **amount**. Add a control point by holding the *Ctrl* key on your keyboard, and click somewhere on the line. You need two control points, one at 0 horizontally and the other at 1.0 horizontally.

17. You can move a control point by holding the *Ctrl* key on your keyboard and dragging the point upwards. Move the first control point up to around 0.25 vertical. Leave the other one unmodified. You now have a curve that begins at the value 0.25 and then fades to the value 0. In other words, it begins with 25 percent opacity and goes to 0 percent throughout its life.

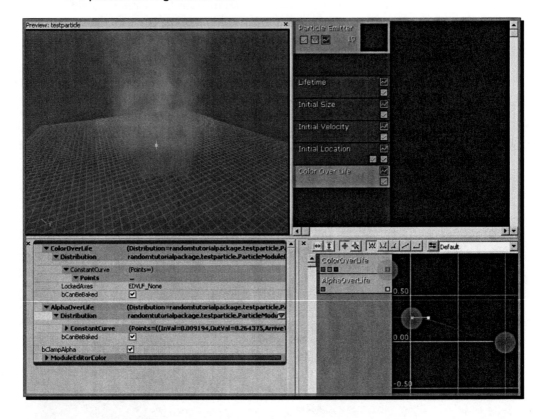

18. The smoke now fades out. To make it fade in, you would need to add a third control point in the middle, and set the first control point back at 0, 0.

19. The last thing to do is to make the particle grow in size. This too is done with the curve editor.

20. Right-click the **Particle Emitter** column in **Area 2** and choose **Size | Size By Life**. Then click on the little scan line button to add the module to the curve editor, like you did for the **ColorOverLife** module as well.

21. Click the little yellow square of the **AlphaOverLife** section in the curve editor to make its curve invisible, as it will only get in your way when working with the size curve.

22. The **LockedAxis** property must be set to **EDVLF_XYZ**, because that gives you just one curve to work with, rather than three.

23. Also, you may need to set the **Distribution** to **DistributionVectorConstantCurve** again, exactly like you did before with the **AlphaOverLife** module.

24. Once you're done with all of that, add two control points to the curve, one at 0 and the other at 1. Move the first one slightly up and the second one much further up.

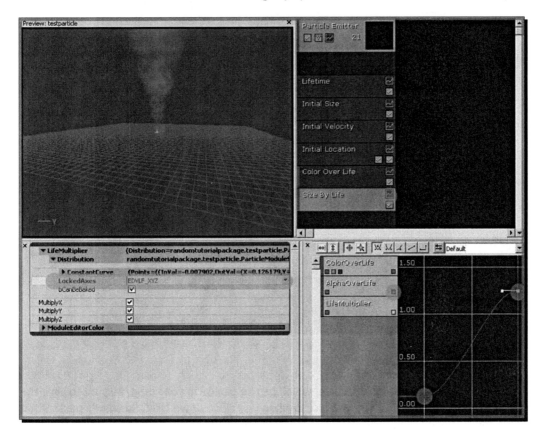

25. You're done! Exit cascade. Be sure to have the particle selected in the generic browser, then right-click a surface in your level and **Add Actor | Add Emitter**.

26. If the particle looks too thin, then add more particles to its SpawnRate. Also, it may be a good idea to add the module **Initial Rotation**, just to give each particle a random rotation, which looks more natural.

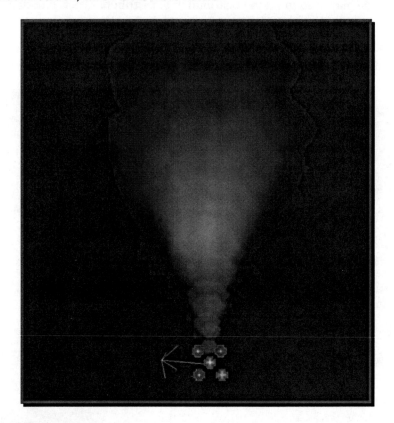

What just happened?

We have now created a smoke particle, which can be placed in your map. Be sure to save the package the particle is in, or you will lose it when you close down UDK. So what's next? What about adding height fog to give our map atmosphere? Let's go ahead and create a height fog particle.

 Contrary to UE3, particles can now be scaled. You can freely scale the draw scale of the particle and the particles will scale accordingly.

Time for action – adding height fog

Height fog is a great way to add atmosphere to your level. It can help set the mood and make distant objects really feel like they're at a distance. You can add height fog to your level by placing a height fog actor as follows:

1. Open your level, go to the **Actor Classes** tab of the generic browser. **HeightFog** can be found under the **Info** category.

2. Select **HeightFog**, then add it to your level (right-click somewhere in the level and choose **Add HeightFog Here**).

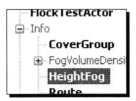

3. You may not notice the effects of the fog right away, especially if you placed the actor on the floor. That's because the position of the height fog actor you just placed controls where the fog starts—if you placed it low (or on the floor), the fog starts too low to affect your level.

4. Grab the **HeightFog** actor and move it up near the ceiling or higher. The fog still isn't very thick, but you should be able to see its effect on the level as the actor moves.

Setting parameters

1. Bring up the properties of the height fog and open up the **HeightFog | Component** category. Let's look at some ways to control the look of the fog.

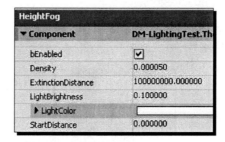

2. Try playing with the **Density** first. This controls how thick the air appears. If you couldn't see the effects of the fog before, you definitely can now.

3. Next, tweak the **LightColor** parameter. The results should be pretty obvious. **LightBrightness** is a multiplier against the **LightColor**, and can make the fog appear brighter or darker. Notice that you can add colored fog, or even black fog for a surreal effect.

4. **StartDistance** controls how far away the fog begins to render. Plugin a **StartDistance** of 300 with a **Density** of 0.05, and you'll see right away how this parameter works.

Uses

You can get a variety of effects out of a **HeightFog** actor. Ultimately, the look you'll want for your fog is tied closely with the lighting and post processing that you apply to your scene, but these examples should give you a good starting point.

Atmospheric haze

Use a low **Density**; a light bluish color, and possibly a high **StartDistance** to make objects in the distance appear hazy. Play with the vertical position of the **HeightFog** actor to tweak the look—placing it high in the air may yield better results.

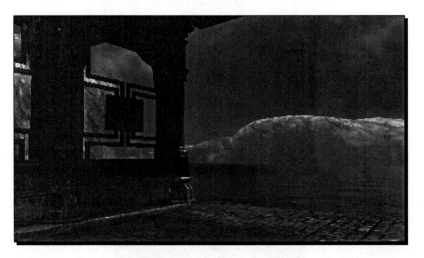

Localized fog

Use a high **Density** combined with a low position to make localized ground fog.

Dense haze

A high **Density** combined with a high position will fill the whole scene with fog, and you can tint the color to give the scene an eerie feeling.

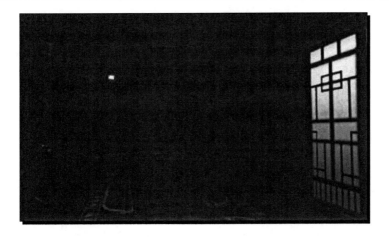

What just happened?

We have created a height fog, but that isn't always the best way to get atmosphere into your scene. It tends to have kind of a flat look, and it's applied evenly to the whole level, which makes it hard to customize for individual areas.

Have a go hero – alternatives to height fog

Spend some time looking at unreal levels that have the kind of atmosphere you want. Open them in the editor. In a lot of cases, you'll see that localized atmosphere effects are created by a static mesh with a custom material applied to it. Some levels have some pretty nifty light beam effects inside. No need to recreate this effect from scratch. Select the mesh and you can copy and paste it into your own map (*Ctrl + C* to copy, *Ctrl + V* to paste).

Look around, and once you know what to look for, you'll see atmospheric meshes everywhere. Reuse anything that you think will fit your level, but be careful, as the quickest way to kill performance is to have too many overlapping atmospheric meshes. Make sure that you can only see through one or two of these meshes at a time, from any camera angle. In other words, don't make a hallway with 30 haze cards staggered down its length.

Time for action – creating the surface

1. Go to the generic browser and find yourself a nice plane. Package **UN_ SimpleMeshes** (loaded by default), has one.

2. Add the plane to the level and position it correctly. You may need to scale it up a lot to make it fit the area.

3. In its properties, expand the section **Collision** and set **CollisionType** to **NoCollision**.

4. Next, expand the section **StaticMeshActor**, then the section **Lighting**, and disable everything.

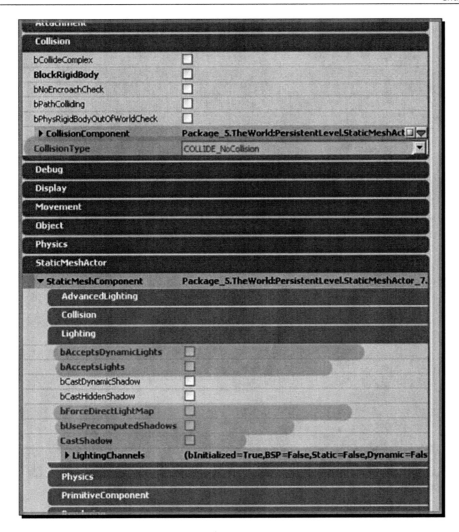

5. Leave the properties window open and return to the generic browser.

6. Find yourself a neat water material. The packages **UN_Liquid** and **UN_Liquid2** would be a good place to start. I personally used material **UN_Liquid.SM.Materials.M_ UN_Liquid_SM_DistortionRiver_01** for this tutorial, even though it is a one-sided material, it is kind of a problem as you will notice later. It is also possible to create your own water materials, but this is quite a complex process, explained in detail in my two water material tutorials. So please refer to those if you plan on doing so.

7. Assign the material to the plane using the **Material** property in the **Rendering** section of the properties of the plane.

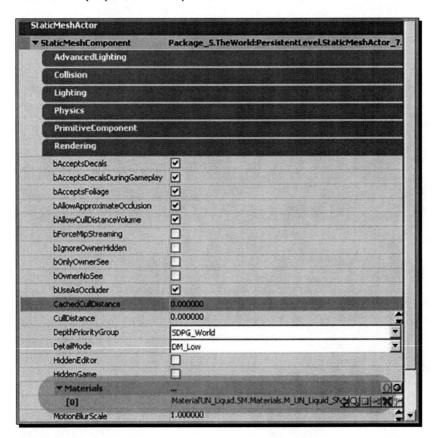

What just happened?

So we have now created the surface dimension for the water to be placed. Let's now go ahead and add the water particle, which will also be swimmable for the player to move about.

Time for action – water volumes

1. Resize the red builder brush so that it covers everything that you wish to flood. It is important to match the top face of the red builder brush exactly with the plane you've just placed, or else the water would actually end at a location other than what the plane would imply. The plane's only use is to visually represent a body of water. The real water, however, is entirely independent of the plane. It would be possible to delete the plane and still have water to swim in, albeit invisible water.

2. Once you have positioned the red builder brush correctly, right-click the volume button on the left toolbar and pick **UTWaterVolume**.

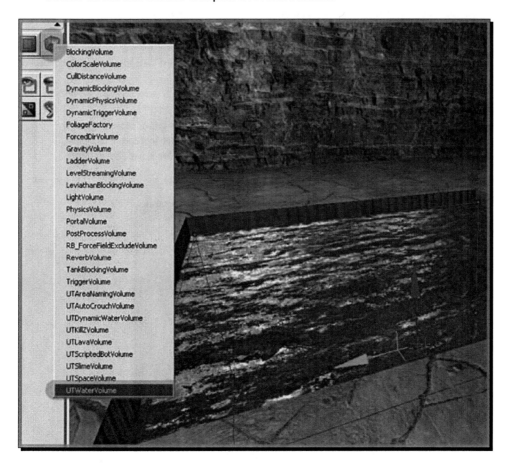

3. Now, move the red builder brush away to reveal the pink water volume below. If you do not see it, you might have toggled volumes off with the *O* key on the keyboard. Your water is now swimmable.

What just happened?

So, we have now completed creating our surface for water, which is also swimmable, but what if we want to make it so that we can swim underwater? Maybe you want to put a special power up underwater for players to grab. I will now show you how to create this underwater particle effect.

Time for action – underwater

As things look different underwater, you want to apply different post-process settings to the area.

1. To do so, make your red builder brush roughly the same size as your water volume and position it at the same location.

 It may help to actually make it slightly smaller or larger than the water volume, as it may be difficult selecting the volume instead, if they are both at the same location. Once you have positioned the red builder brush correctly, add a **PostProcessVolume**.

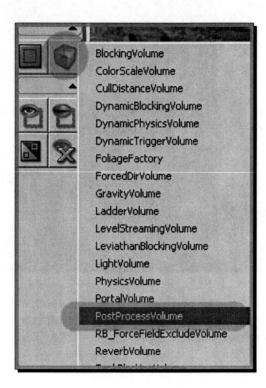

2. You now have two volumes around your body of water. Select the **PostProcessVolume** you've just added, and open up its properties.

3. Expand the **PostProcessVolume** section and configure the properties marked in the following screenshot:

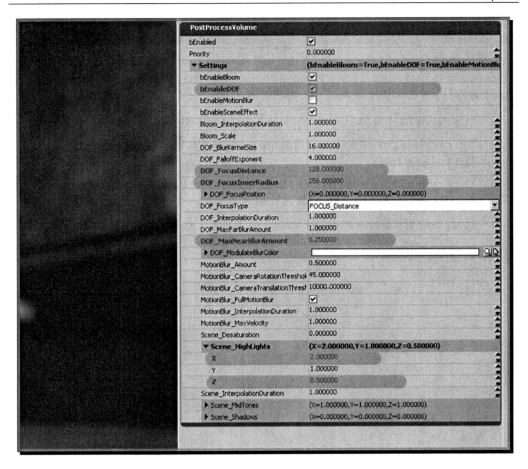

4. By enabling **bEnableDOF**, you enabled the depth of field, causing the water to blur your vision, which you further tweaked with **DOF_FocusDistance**, **DOF_FocusInnerRadius**, and **DOF_MaxNearBlurAmount**. Also, by changing **Scene_Highlights X** to **2.000000** and **Z** to **0.500000**, you gave the water a blue overlay.

5. Experiment all you like with these settings, as you can accomplish some great effects using them.

What just happened?

You are done! Additionally, you can also add a **HeightFog** actor to simulate depth in the body of water, but this will work only if the water is at the lowest point of the level, otherwise the fog would also cover other areas of the level, and you obviously don't want that. A fog volume might bring relief in such a case (**Actor | Info | FogVolumeDensityInfo**). Lava, slime, and the others are all handled in the same way.

Have a go hero – animated cloud shadows

First, you need to create a cloud texture that will work for your scene. For this I used the **clouds** option in Photoshop. I know that the Photoshop filters can be terrible; however, I'll explain why I used this filter instead of creating my own.

- ◆ The **clouds** filter in Photoshop creates a seamless texture to work with.

- ◆ You can press *Ctrl + F* on your keyboard until you get the result you want, and it is fast and easy to do.

- ◆ The way in which we will be using these textures is by adding them together within the UT3 shader network to achieve the result we are looking for.

- ◆ Every time you create a texture using this, it is soft and gradient. Later on, we will be controlling the sharp edges and how they fall off, their brightness and their shadows.

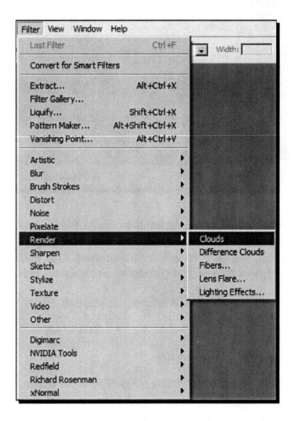

This is the image that I created using Photoshop:

Now, to create a light material.

1. In the general browser window, right-click and create **New Material**.

2. Bring in your texture and hook it up to the **Emissive** channel in your material.

3. Lights do not lighten the scene with the diffuse map, but rather determine the strength of the light. Think of any color you can. This color cannot exist unless there is a light strength value, that is what the **Emissive** channel does for lights.

4. Select the material itself (image, for example, **Previewmaterial_6**), and under **Lighting** model, select **MLM_Unlit**, scroll down and check off **Bused As Light Function** (first option under **Usage**).

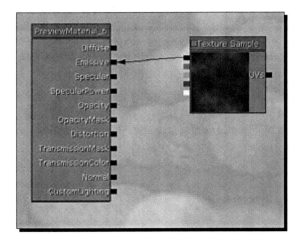

5. Next, you will need to plug this material into your light channel. With your light selected, press *F4* on your keyboard, navigate under the **Light** submenu until you see **Function**. To the right, you will see a blue arrow pointing down. Press that and the **Light Function**, which drops down after it.

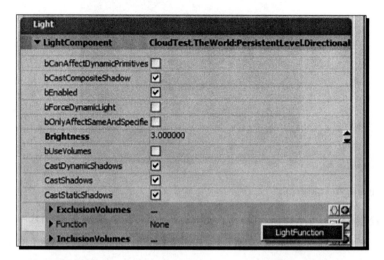

6. After selecting **Light Function**, you should see the following screenshot:

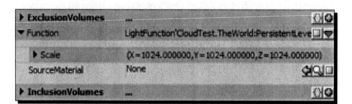

7. With your light material selected, click on the green arrow pointing left beside **Source Material**. You're done; your material is hooked up.

   If you are making an outdoor scene, make sure you plug your material into the light, which casts the shadows for your scene. The reason for doing this is so that the shadows of the buildings and the shadows you are creating for the clouds match exactly.

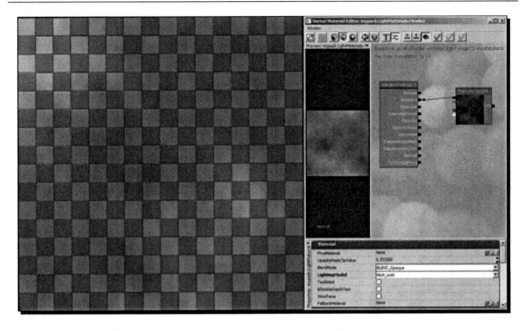

Yes, it will look nothing like clouds, and it will not animate, this is just the first step to see how the light works with your scene.

8. Next, we will be animating the light to get an idea of the speed and angle we want. We first do this instead of overlaying the clouds, because both the clouds will be moving in roughly the same direction, with a slightly different speed and angle to add variation, plus we need to see how the cloud textures play with one another in the editor when it is being animated, not when it is stationary.

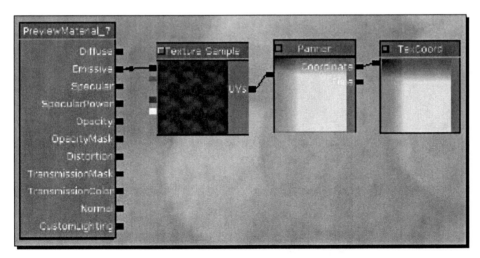

9. To animate your texture, add a **Panner** and **TexCoord** to your scene.

10. The **TexCoord** is only used to scale up or down your texture in the scene; the **Panner** is used to translate the texture.

   For the **Panner** value, I set my angle and speed to **SpeedX** – 0.01,**SpeedY** – 0.05.

 The settings you plug into **Panner** is directly related to the rotation of your light, so if you want the angle of the shadows translation to change, then you can toy around with the different variables in **Panner**, or simply rotate your light. Make sure you rotate it using **local** settings, so that the global angle does not change and the shadows fall in the exact same way. Also, for a directional light, the height of the light itself does not affect the shadows scale.

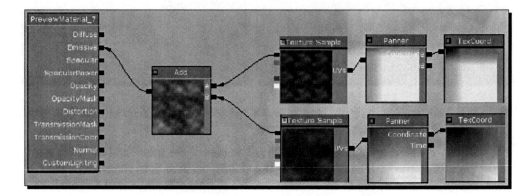

11. Next, you will need to duplicate the texture—**Panner** and **TexCoord** nodes in the material shader—and plug both into an **Add** node, which then plugs into the **Emissive**.

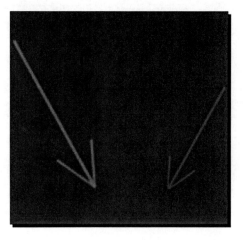

12. The second texture should have a different setting in **TexCoord**, and the direction should be slightly different so that they are not moving in the exact same direction. With these slight changes, the clouds will soon have much more variation, as well as a lot less repeating (mainly due to the scale of the textures).

13. Do not scale your clouds down by half; find a value that does not go into the size of your original texture scale. For example, if the first is set to repeat three times, the second should be around `0.85` or `1.35`. They will have to repeat a bit more often to multiply into each other, resulting in variation.

14. As of now, there is more variation. However, we will want to tighten the gaps and adjust the light and dark areas a bit more to achieve a better result.

    To do this, we will need to add a **Lerp** and two **constant** variables to the scene. Plug the **Add** variable into the `alpha` of your **Lerp**, and each constant goes into **A** and **B**. What this will do is, the black-and-white cloud textures will be multiplied by the **A** and **B** values. For this example, I set the constant plugged into the **Lerp A** channel to **-1**, and the constant plugged into **Lerp B** was set to **3**. The **Lerp** is then plugged into the **Emissive**.

However, a problem might come up. When dealing with a **Lerp**, you can only have a black-and-white channel to drive the alpha, so you will need to plug the red, green, or blue channels of the cloud textures into the **Add** variable, instead of the entire texture.

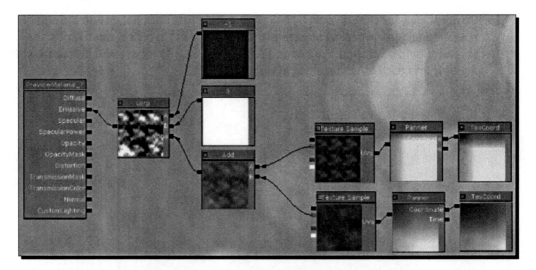

15. The previous screenshot is the result that you should achieve with these updates. A lot closer to more realistic clouds. However, there is one big issue. If you look at the clouds before this last change, there is not a lot of detail; however, it does not glow. This last step amplified the colors, and the more they are apart from each other (currently by a total of four) the more extreme they become, and the tighter the shadows and light areas are.

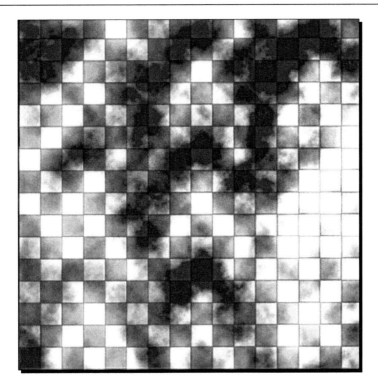

The previous screenshot has the constant variables set to 12 and -4, four times as high as the last one. As you can see, the clouds are much tighter, but the lit areas are much brighter.

The shadow color does not change, because you cannot get a shadow darker than 100 percent black and the fill lights to lighten these areas, so no matter how dark you make this light, these shadows will always be this dark. To adjust these, change the fill lights.

16. The best way to fix this issue is to balance your constant variables, so the white is not too bright, but if you want a larger gap between shadows, sometimes there's no other way, but to set this value high.

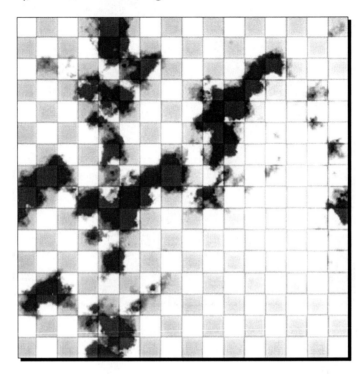

17. The other way to fix this is to create a **Clamp** and two more constant variables. The **Lerp** should be plugged into the first channel on the **Clamp**, each constant into the **Min** and **Max** channel, and the **Clamp** into the **Emissive**. What this **Clamp** does is literally clamp the value to the **Min** and **Max** settings. Keep **Min** at 0, but change the constant plugged into **Max** to 1.

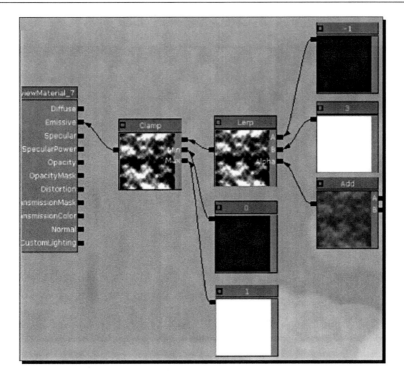

18. When you save the material, you won't see any change right away, but when you change it to **0.75**, **0.5**, or **0.25**, you notice a big change, especially the lower you go.

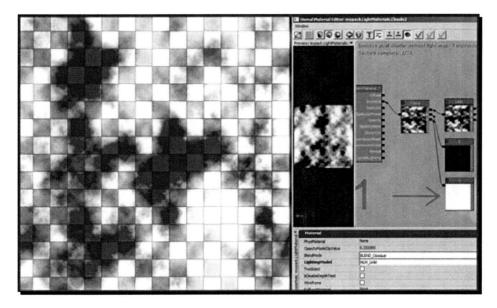

19. The following screenshot shows how it appears when set to 0.75:

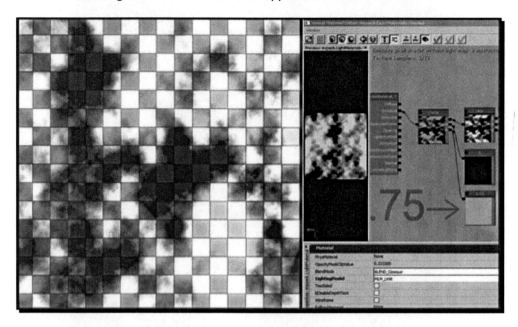

20. The following screenshot shows how it appears when set to 0.5:

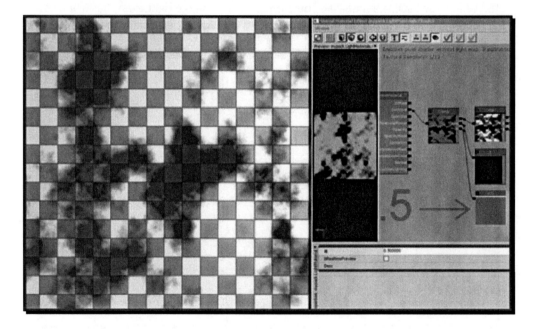

21. The following screenshot shows how it appears when set to `0.25`:

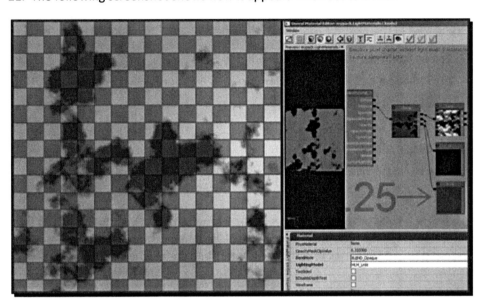

Since the ground is white and grey to begin with, in this example it is hard to tell exactly how it will affect your environment, but a good way to see the changes in this image is the material preview box. As the white color is lowered, it does not lower everything uniformly, it simply clamps the color at that value based on the texture, so you will lose detail in the transition from light to shaded, creating a harder shadow edge (usually more pixelated), so be careful when tweaking this value.

Pop quiz

In the cascade **Particle Editor**, which area is the property section that will display the properties of whatever emitter or module is selected in the **Particle Editor**?

1. Area 1
2. Area 2
3. Area 3
4. Area 4

Summary

We learned a lot in this chapter about the following:

- The basics of the cascade particle editor
- How to add a new particle emitter
- How to create a smoke effect using the particle editor
- How to add height fog
- Creating a surface
- How to create water volumes
- Creating swimmable water

We have learnt how to incorporate different particle systems into your map, such as smoke, fog, and water. In the next chapter, we will be looking into movement with movers using triggers, emitters, and volumes to activate elevators and doors when walking past them.

5
Movement with Movers

In this chapter, we will introduce you to the world of animated level geometry in UDK, doors, elevators, and so on, activated using InterpActors or triggers. This section will look at creating a basic elevator/door with UT's unique style. We will look at how to continuously loop and rotate animations, and how to attach certain objects to the elevator/door.

In this chapter, we shall cover the following topics:

- ◆ A basic elevator/door
- ◆ Elevators UT style
- ◆ A continuously looping animation
- ◆ A continuously rotating animation
- ◆ Attaching something

Lock and Load!

Let's first have a look at creating a basic elevator/door consisting of a moving plateau; call it an elevator if you want and assign an InterpActor to it.

Time for action – a basic elevator/door

1. The first thing you need to do is select the static mesh you wish to use in the content browser, then right-click somewhere in a viewport, and add it as an InterpActor:

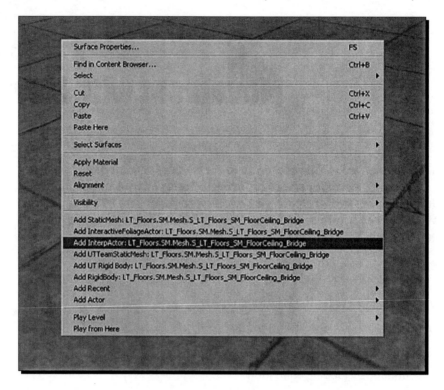

2. Next, open up Kismet. A button with a green **K** in the top toolbar:

3. Keep the InterpActor you just made selected in the viewport. Then in the Kismet window, right-click the large empty gray space in the middle and click **New Matinee**:

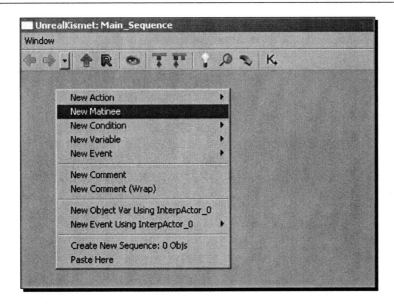

4. A **Matinee** block is added. Double-click this block to open the **Matinee** sub-editor. Right-click in the dark gray space in the center-left of this window and click **Add New Empty Group**:

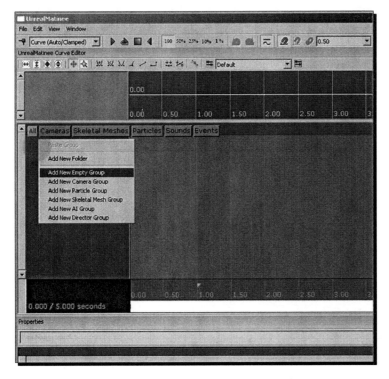

5. Right-click the **NewGroup** that you just made and then click **Add New Movement Track**:

6. Move the timeline to another position; in my example, it was moved to 3 seconds by clicking in the dark gray space at the bottom of the timeline. Press *Enter* to add a key to the current position. Keys are positions that the engine remembers. Note how you can increase or decrease the length of the matinee by clicking-and-dragging the small orange triangle at the bottom right. In my example, it is located at 4.5 seconds:

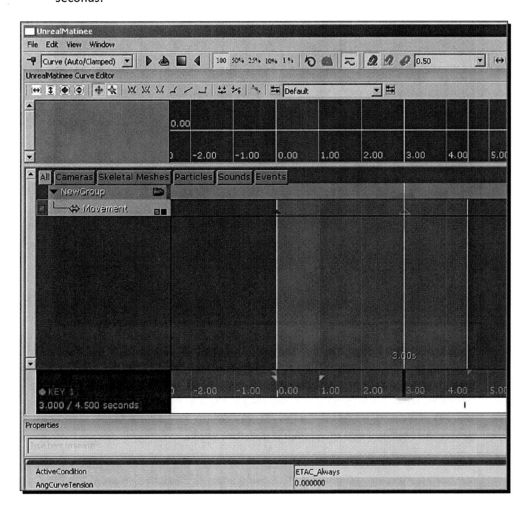

7. Keys are displayed as small dark red triangles. Select the one you just added, if it is not already, and then while keeping this **Matinee** window open, go back to your viewport. Move the InterpActor the normal way, using the movement gizmo, and as soon as you moved it somewhere and let go of the mouse, you should see a yellow line appearing. This is the path the InterpActor will follow between its first position and the new position you just added:

Note how it says **Adjust Key 1** at the bottom-left of the viewport. If this does not show up, you did not select the key in **Matinee**. Also, if no yellow line shows up, then the InterpActor may not be properly associated with the **Matinee** you made. It is critical that the InterpActor is selected in the viewport throughout the entire process of creating a **Matinee**, a new **Empty Group**, and a **New Movement Track**. Delete the **Matinee** and try again if it does not work.

8. Return to the **Matinee** window, then click-and-drag the timeline around. You should see the InterpActor in the viewport moving around. You can also press the **Play** button at the top of the **Matinee** window to play your animation.

9. Next, we are going to add a trigger so the player can activate the animation in-game. Right-click somewhere and click **Add Actor | Add Trigger**:

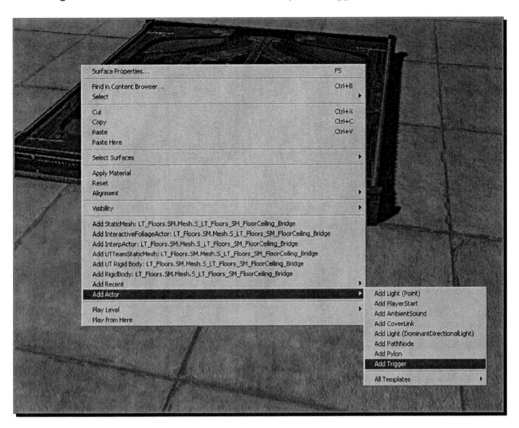

10. Select the trigger and go to Kismet. Right-click somewhere near the **Matinee** and click **New Event Using Trigger_0 | Touch**:

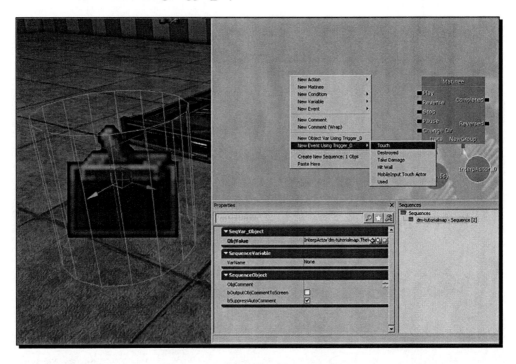

11. Connect **Touched** to **Play** and connect the **Completed** to its own **Reverse** in **Matinee**. This will make the platform return automatically, as soon as it reaches the end of its animation. Also note how I set **MaxTriggerCount** to **0** in the properties of the **Trigger_0 Touch** event:

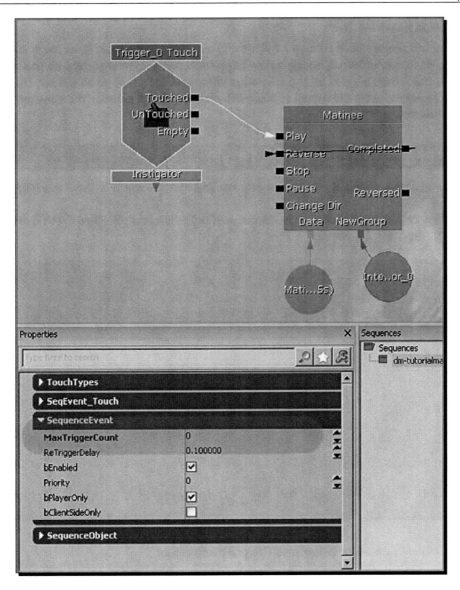

12. That's it! You are done. As soon as you touch the trigger, the platform will play its animation.

Movement with Movers

What just happened?

So, as you can see, we have created a full moving elevator using a basic static mesh and assigning an InterpActor to it, which is then triggered when someone steps onto the platform, and it then triggers off the animation lifting you. Let's now go ahead and create a matinee sequence using the unreal matinee browser, which will animate the elevator, making it move.

Time for action – elevators UT style

A special setup is available for UT style elevators. This method works without any triggers.

1. Select your InterpActor, go to Kismet, and right-click and pick **New Event Using InterpActor_0 | Mover**:

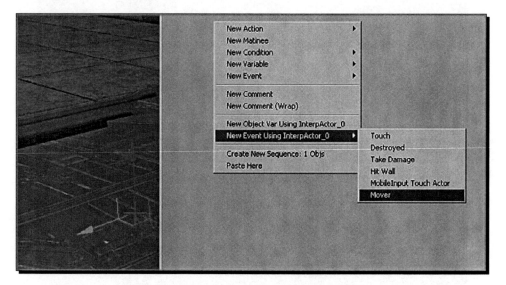

2. You will now automatically get this pre-made setup:

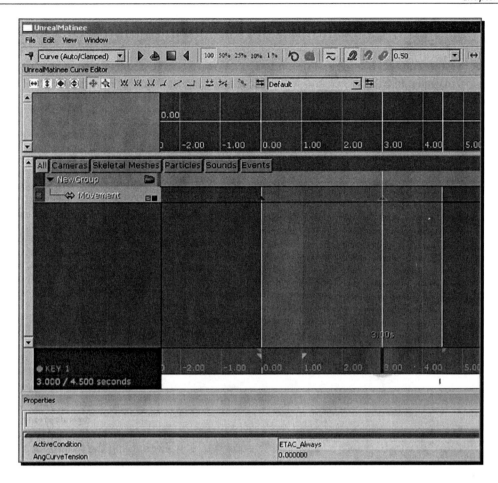

3. Simply open up the **Matinee** window and animate it the regular way, and you are done.

What just happened?

So, now we have a matinee sequence created in unreal matinee browser, which animates the elevator to move. But what if want it to loop over and over again? Let's now go ahead and have a look at how we can continuously loop the matinee animation.

Time for action – a continuously looping animation

1. Simply connect Matinee's **Completed** to its own **Reverse** and its **Reverse** to **Play**. This will make it go back-and-forth forever, as soon as it is triggered once, by an external event:

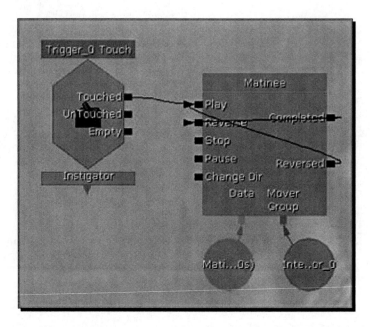

2. Another way to create a looping animation is by simply enabling the **bLooping** property found in the **Matinee** block in **Kismet**. Both approaches will roughly get you the same result.

What just happened?

So, we now have a continuously looping animation for our elevator, but what if we want a rotating animation for, say, a door or a drawbridge? Let's now go ahead and have a look at how we can continuously rotate the matinee's animation.

Time for action – a continuously rotating animation

You could use **Matinee** to make a rotating animation, but it is usually easier to go with the old-school approach and simply do it all through the properties of the InterpActor.

1. Open up those properties and navigate to the **Movement** section. Set **Physics** to **PHYS_Rotating** and set a value to **RotationRate**:

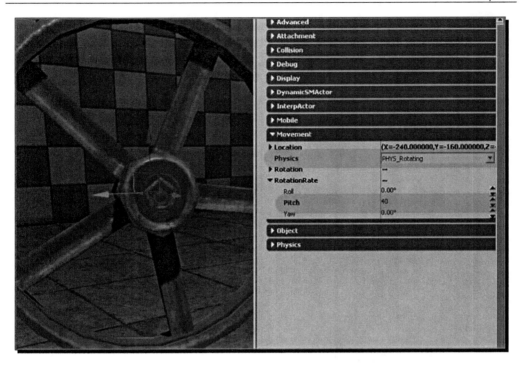

2. The value set in **RotationRate** is the degrees it will rotate in 1 second.

What just happened?

So, we now have a continuously rotating animation which can be used to rotate anything from an elevator, door, or even a drawbridge; so what's next? How about attaching something, for example, a light? Let's see how we can do this by using a dynamic version of a InterpActor.

Time for action – attaching something

1. If you want to attach, for example, a light to an InterpActor, you first of all need to make sure that you have a dynamic version of the actor that you wish to attach. In my example, it can be found in the **Actor Browser | Lights | PointLights | PointLightMovable**. Remember that some actors are static and cannot be moved, and thus cannot be attached.

2. Next, open up the properties of whatever actor you want to attach, and navigate to **Attachment**. Enter the name of the actor you want to attach to in **Base**. In my case, my InterpActor is called **InterpActor_0**, so I typed that in **Base** and hit *Enter*, and I got something similar to the following screenshot:

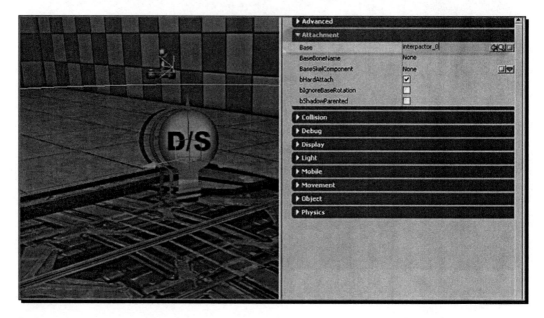

What just happened?

So, now we have light on our elevator, which makes it look more ideal. You can pretty much attach anything to give the mover purpose or meaning, for example, putting a switch on an elevator, which is then activated/triggered when the player interacts with it.

Have a go hero – triggering sounds

The sound cue route requires you to add a play sound action to Kismet.

1. Right-click in **Kismet | Action | Sound | Play Sound** or hold *s* on the keyboard and click somewhere. In its properties, you then enter the desired sound cue. Also, you must set an actor as the target for the sound, or it wouldn't know where it needs to be located. Failure of specifying an actor, while it will work, can lead to problems later on. Playing too many sounds on the same actor can also lead to problems.

2. Select the actor you wish to use; in my example, it was an **Emitter**. Right-click in **Kismet**, pick **New Object Var Using "NameOfActor"**, and connect it to **Target**. You're done. There's not more to it than that.

   The following set up plays a sound, once a **Matinee** sequence (could be an elevator or a door) has completed. It uses an emitter as its source/target:

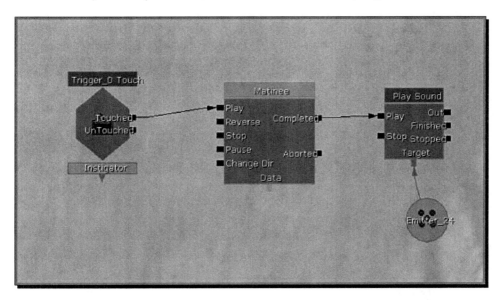

3. Alternatively, you can also trigger a normal sound through **Kismet**. To do so, add an **AmbientSoundSimpleToggleable**, which is found under **AmbientSoundSimple** in the actor browser. Add it to the level and add the sound you want to play to its properties:

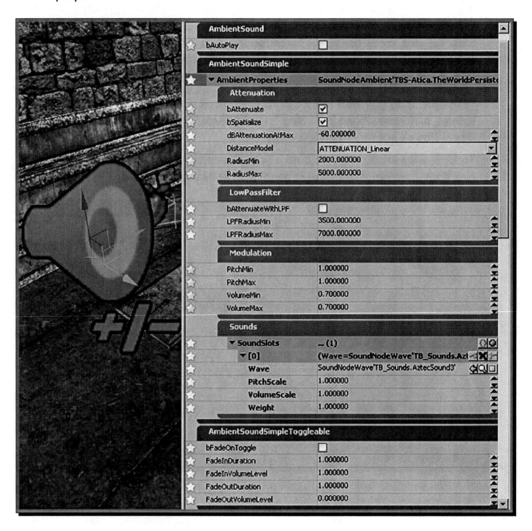

A number of new properties are available in this actor:

- ❑ **BAutoPlay**: Whether the sound should start by itself or not
- ❑ **BFadeOnToggle**: Whether the sound should fade in and out
- ❑ **Fade Duration and Volume**: How fast it should fade in and out

4. Next, open **Kismet** and add a **Toggle** action by clicking on **New Action | Toggle | Toggle** or hold *t* on the keyboard and click somewhere.

5. Define the **AmbientSoundSimpleToggleable** as the **Target**, and toggle it on and off. If you don't toggle it off, the sound will continue to play, so toggle it off. For example, if the sound is 3.45 seconds long, toggle it off after 3.45 seconds:

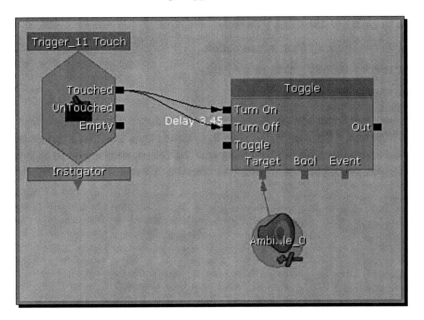

Pop quiz

What does the button with a green **K** in the top toolbar stand for?

Summary

We learned a lot in this chapter.

Specifically, we covered the following:

- How to create a basic elevator/door
- How to create an elevators UT's style
- How to continuously loop an animation
- How to continuously rotate an animation
- How to attach something

At this point, you now know how to create elevators and doors, which will be activated when something is triggered, if the player stands on it, or if the player is within a certain radius. You can also make movers more life-like by adding emitters (water, smoke, and so on)and sounds. In the next chapter, we will be looking at terrain and the different types of layers used.

6
Terrain

Unreal Engine 3 supports a flexible terrain system that provides a wide variety of visual styles and uses. Many different landscapes can be realized and various themes can be achieved utilizing a heightmap based system that can visually depict hills, valleys, mountains, rivers, roads, and more. It can also depict a multi-layer terrain material system that supports real-world texture files such as dirt, rock, sand, and mud.

A multi-layer decoration system provides additional flexibility and realism by rendering foliage such as grass, weeds, bushes, flowers, and even small rocks and debris.

Terrain is typically created using one of the two techniques: hand-painting directly on the terrain mesh to create the hills and valleys, or importing externally created terrain height maps. Additionally, height map information can be acquired from **Digital Elevation Model** *(DEM) information. Material layers that represent dirt, grass, and rocks can be created using terrain alpha maps that determine where the texture is blended onto the terrain.*

In this chapter, we shall cover the following topics:

- ◆ Your first terrain
- ◆ Applying materials
- ◆ Light mapping

So, let's get on with it.

Terrain creation in UDK is a little different than it was in UE2. The process has been simplified and you no longer need to manually create the alpha maps for the terrain. The terrain editing mode interface has also been updated, and now it features a whole bunch of new tools. The terrain now also supports deco layers with collision and lighting, terrain LODing, light mapping, and automatic texturing based on the angle and height of the surface. For this section, we will only focus on the basic process of setting up a terrain and a bit of information on its light mapping.

Time for action – your first terrain

Before you add a terrain to a level, be sure to have saved the level at least once, as the terrain will attempt to save itself within the level, for which the level has to **exist** in the first place.

1. Open the generic browser. If it isn't already open, go to the **Actors** tab, expand the **Uncategorized** section and select the actor **Terrain**, as shown in the following screenshot:

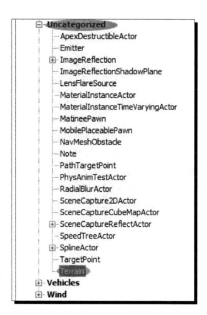

2. In the viewport, hold down *a* on your keyboard, and click a surface in your level to add the **Terrain** actor at that location. Your terrain should show up as shown in the following screenshot; tiny, and with a default texture applied.

3. Let's expand it. New for Unreal Engine 3 is the ability to expand a terrain whenever you want. You are no longer restricted to the original size as you were in Unreal Engine 2. Double-click the terrain in the viewport to have its properties pop up. You should preferably also set the viewport to wireframe to get a better view on what's going on:

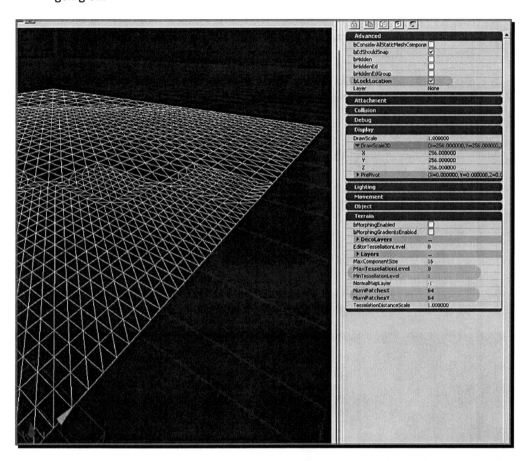

NumPatches X and **NumPatchesY** in the **Terrain** section control the actual size of the terrain. Changing those values will increase both the size and the complexity of the terrain. By default, a terrain is 4×4 patches large or small; you should increase those values to something like 64×64 or 256×256 for large outdoor levels. You should consider modifying the drawscale of the terrain if you want to increase the terrain even further. Simply adding more patches to increase the size is usually a bad idea, as it can have a significant impact on performance.

As you can see in the following screenshot, my terrain also LODs itself. The LODing strength is controlled by **MaxTesselationLevel**, **MinTesselationLevel**, and **TesselationDistanceScale**. A higher **Max** means more aggressive LODing, whereas the **DistanceScale** controls the distance. A higher value in **DistanceScale** also means more aggressive LODing.

4. Lastly, you may also want to enable **LockLocation** under the **Advanced** section, so as to not accidentally move the terrain while editing the level. This will color the **Terrain** actor red.

5. Next, open up the **Terrain Editing Mode** window. This is found on the left toolbar, right below the standard camera button:

6. In the window that pops up, you can find all the tools that you need for modifying the terrain. I have highlighted the six most important tools:

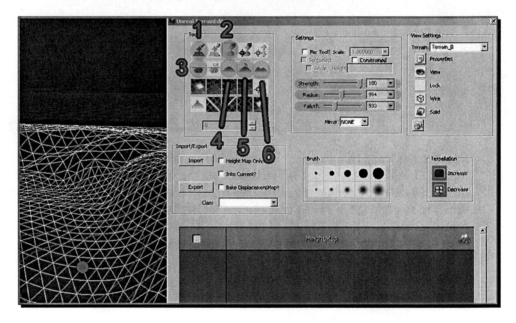

1. Let's you extend the edges of the terrain. It basically does the same as altering **NumPatches** in the properties window.

2. The standard paint tool raises or lowers the terrain and paints or un-paints texture and foliage layers.

3. Flattens the area based on the height of the vertex where the operation started. Everything is raised or lowered to the height of the vertex where you started dragging.

4. Smoothens the area. Also works for blurring texture layers.

5. Flattens an area using its average height.

6. Adds noise to either the geometry or texturing of the terrain.

All of these are controlled by the **Strength:**, **Radius:**, and **Falloff:** sliders. Pre-sets are available in the **Brush** section, although, I personally find those rather useless.

Any of these tools can be used by holding *Ctrl* on your keyboard and dragging the mouse over the terrain while holding the left or right mouse button. A right-click usually does the opposite of a left-click. For example, left-clicking will raise the terrain and right-clicking will lower the terrain again.

7. If the **Strength, Radius,** or **Falloff** sliders are not powerful enough for you, it is also possible to manually type in a value in the text field next to the sliders, to further bump up their power. This is especially handy for huge terrains that require large brushes to get around:

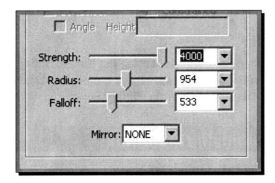

8. Another handy tool is the visibility tool, as shown in the following screenshot:

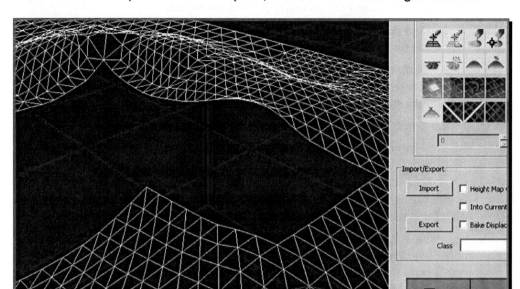

By dragging over the terrain, this tool lets you hide blocks of terrain. This is ideal if you want to get rid of the terrain in a specific location, for example, if you want to add a basement to a building, or to optimize the terrain. Areas that can never be seen by the player should preferably be hidden with this tool.

What just happened?

So, we have created the shape of our terrain using the terrain editing tool. The next step is to apply a material to the terrain to make it look more atmospheric and life-like. I will now show you how to apply a material using the terrain editing browser.

Time for action – applying materials

Let's add textures/materials to the terrain.

1. Switch the viewport back to a textured view and go to the generic browser. Find a material that you like, select it in the generic browser, and return to the **Terrain Editing Mode** window.

2. In the **Terrain Editing Mode** window, right-click the big empty space at the bottom, below where it says **Height Map**, pick **New Layer from material (auto-create)**, and enter a name.

3. Select another material in the generic browser, and do this one more time so you have two layers as shown in the next screenshot. If it asks for a package and layer name, as some versions do (UT3), ensure that your package name is the same as your level name, to embed the material information inside the level itself. UDK will ask for a name twice: one for **TerrainLayerSetup** and one for **Terrain Material**. Enter two different names for the two, but the same package name. If your level is named Layouttest754, your package too should be named the same. The layer name itself doesn't matter a lot. Pick anything, but remember that names must be unique and without spaces and all:

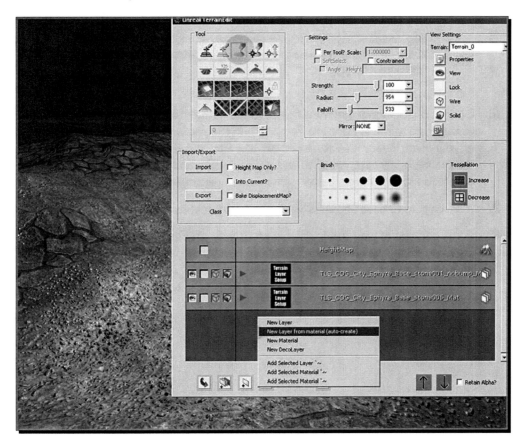

4. The first layer will automatically display on the terrain as it is the first, therefore always visible. The second layer, however, will remain invisible until you paint it.

Select the second layer by clicking it (it turns yellow as shown in the previous screenshot), and select the standard paint tool with which you modified the geometry of the terrain, and start painting away.

If the editor refuses to let you paint materials on the terrain, it might help to move the entire terrain a bit, or to expand it, or to restart the editor. After you've moved it at least once, it seems to wake up and allow painting. You may need to temporarily disable **LockLocation**

5. If your terrain turns funky after you've added several different layers, you need to replace the materials with simpler materials. You can add as many materials as you want.

 Any additional layer will impact performance. Adding dozens of layers is therefore not really advised. Four to six or so, should do for most large and outdoor levels.

6. Options of additional materials can be found in the properties of every layer. To get to these, go to the generic browser and find the package that has the same name as your level. If your level is named `DM-Forest`, you should look for a package with that name. In my case, my level was not saved yet, and it generated a `Package_0` name. You should have a better name than my example.

7. Also, be sure to have **Show All Resource Types** enabled at the top-left.

8. In the package of your level, which is effectively your level itself (think of it as a package inside a level—**Mylevel** for those familiar with UE1 and 2), you should see all kinds of assets related to your terrain:

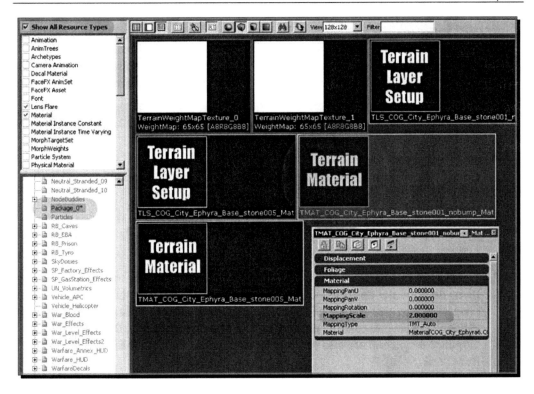

9. Open a **Terrain Material** asset by right-clicking **Properties** to get to the **MappingScale** option, which controls the scale of the material. Other neat options are **MappingPan U** and **MappingPanV**, which allow you to offset a material, and **Rotation**, allowing you to rotate-offset the material. **MappingType** allows you to change the axis of the mapping; you may need to change this, if you have a very vertical terrain.

Terrain Layer Setup assets gives you options to enable automatic texturing, based on the angle and height of a surface.

10. If you want to change the material applied to a terrain later on, you can do so by altering **Material** in **Terrain Material**, or by right-clicking an expanded layer in the **Terrain Editing Mode** window, and picking **Use Selected**.

Your change may not show up immediately, and may require you to restart the editor, or use the **RM** button in the **Terrain Editing Mode** window (right side, below the **Wire** and **Solid** buttons) to force the engine to reload the terrain.

What just happened?

So, we have now applied a material to our terrain using the terrain browser. So what is next in terms of terrain? What about lighting? The terrain is already light-mapped in UDK; so, using the terrain properties, I will now show you how to add lighting to your terrain.

Have a go hero – deco layers

Deco Layers are set up in a similar fashion.

1. Open up the properties of the terrain itself by simply double-clicking its surface anywhere in the level, and navigate to **Terrain | Deco** layers.

2. Add an item to it and then add yet another item to decorations. Then add **StaticMeshComponentFactory** to it, and correctly set the **StaticMesh** and other relevant properties.

3. Just like the foliage layers, you are not required to add materials to the **Deco** layers. If you do not enter any material, it will use the one assigned to **StaticMesh**. The properties also give you access to some obvious properties such as **CastShadow**, **Hidden**, and several collision properties. The **Min** and **MaxScale**, **Density**, and **SlopeRotationBlend** are also very similar to the ones found in foliage layers, as is the **RandSeed** (Seed).

 The density should be set quite high, a number like 20 should do. Also, a name can be entered at the top of the **Deco** layers section, if you desire so.

4. Once you've set that up, open the **Terrain Edit** window, select the **Deco** layer in the layers list, and start painting it as if it were a regular terrain material.

It should show up wherever you paint it.

Time for action – light mapping

1. Unlike Unreal Engine 2, terrain is light mapped now. However, if the quality of the light map is not satisfactory enough, it is possible to bump up its quality. To do so, open up the properties of the terrain and expand the **Lighting** section. Enable **bIsOverridingLightResolution**, and enter a higher value under **StaticLightingResolution**.

 This can have quite a performance impact; so again, use it wisely.

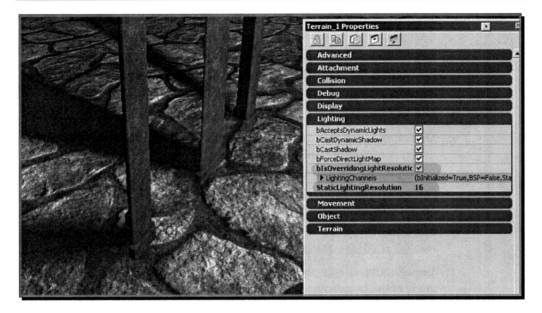

What just happened?

We have assigned a light map to the terrain so when static meshes are introduced to our map and light hits the meshes, we will get dynamic shadowing, giving a more atmospheric approach to our map.

Have a go hero – foliage layers

Foliage layers are embedded into regular terrain material layers, and are thus linked to the material. Paint another material over the one that contains the foliage layer, and the foliage layer too will disappear.

1. In the generic browser, browse to the terrain material of the layer of choice, usually found within the **Mylevel** package of the level, and double-click it to get to its properties. Expand **Foliage** and add an item to **FoliageMeshes** using the little plus button. The following properties would be found:

   ❏ **StaticMesh**: What static mesh it will use for the foliage layer. A **grass** mesh would do well.

   ❏ **Material**: This property is optional. If you leave it empty, it will use the material specified in the properties of **StaticMesh**. If you fill something, it will override it.

   ❏ **Density**: How many times **StaticMesh** is instanced. A number like 3 would be a good start.

- ❑ **MaxDrawRadius**: At what distance the foliage meshes should start disappearing, for performance reasons. A couple of thousand should do.

- ❑ **MinTransitionRadius**: Until what distance the foliage meshes should be displayed in full scale. The bigger the difference between **MaxDrawRadius** and **MinTransitionRadius**, the softer the fade out. Can be left at 0.

- ❑ **Min and MaxScale**: The size of the foliage meshes.

- ❑ **Seed**: Can be left at 0. Other numbers will randomize the placement of the foliage meshes differently.

- ❑ **SwayScale**: In combination with the **WindDirectionalSource** actor (see **Foliage Volume** tutorial), this controls the amount of influence the wind has on the foliage meshes.

- ❑ **AlphaMapThreshold**: A higher value will make it spawn less or no foliage meshes at all near the edges of the painted area.

- ❑ **SlopeRotationBlend**: The rotation of the foliage meshes, dependent on the angle of the terrain quad below.

2. If you did all of this correctly, the meshes should show up wherever the material is painted. In my test scenario, it got me a beautiful landscape of springs.

Pop quiz

What are the several different types of properties for refining your mover?

Summary

We learned a lot in this chapter about the following:

- ◆ Creating a terrain in our map
- ◆ Applying materials to our terrain
- ◆ Adding a light map to our terrain

We have learnt how to build a basic terrain, how to apply materials to that terrain, making it more atmospheric and giving it character. We also know how to add light mapping to our terrain, which give us dynamic shadowing when static meshes are introduced to our map. In the next chapter we will start adding items and look into bot placement.

7
Adding Gameplay Elements into your Map

This section explains how to get all of the basic gameplay elements into your map. In this example, we'll set up a Deathmatch map, which is the easiest type to create. Capture the Flag, Warfare maps, and vehicle variants, which have a couple of additional node types that you need to add, are discussed at the end of this tutorial.

In this chapter, we will cover:

- ◆ Naming your map
- ◆ Adding a player start
- ◆ Play in editor
- ◆ Placing pickups
- ◆ Placing weapons
- ◆ Placing jump pads
- ◆ Adding other game objective types
- ◆ Adding path nodes

So let's get on with it...

Let's start by looking into gameplay elements.

Adding gameplay elements

When starting a level, no matter what the game-type is, it is always best to shell out the gameplay before you start on any visual work. With BSP and very few static meshes, quickly flush out the entire level to a point where you can play the level and see how much fun it is. If it's not fun before visual work, it's not going to be fun after, and since visual work in UDK can take the bulk of the level work time, you want to be sure that you get to your level as much fun as possible before you start. So you don't waste a lot of time re-meshing and lighting to accommodate game-play changes.

Time for action – naming your map

First off, naming conventions are important. They're the primary way that UDK knows what type of map you're playing.

1. Start your map name with one of the following tags, depending on the intended gameplay type:

   ❏ **Deathmatch, Team Deathmatch, Duel (DM)**

   ❏ **Capture the Flag (CTF)**

   ❏ **Vehicle Capture the Flag (VCTF)**

   ❏ **Warfare (WAR)**

   So, if you want to make a Warfare map called **FirePits,** you'd name it WAR-FirePits.udk.

2. For this tutorial, we'll create a Deathmatch map. Start by creating a new map or opening an existing map you've created. Save it as DM-GameplayTest01.udk in the following folder:

   C:\UDK\UDK-VersionRelease\UDKGame\Content\Maps

   This is the official place where Unreal likes to look for maps, so get into the habit of saving everything there. If you put the map somewhere else, especially if you're streaming or loading separate packages, Unreal won't be able to find it. If you want to make a subfolder, that's fine too.

3. Build-up your map so that it has at least three rooms connected by hallways, and that they're not in a straight line, as shown in the following screenshot:

If you name it properly, Unreal will recognize this as a Deathmatch map, and once we place the proper actors, Unreal will let you play it as a Deathmatch, Team Deathmatch, or Duel map.

What just happened?

So, we know what the convention is for naming the different types of maps, for example, we know that if we wanted to create a death match level, we would call up our DM and if we wanted a Capture the Flag level, we would name it CTF and if you wanted a Vehicle Capture the Flag, it would be named VCTF. Let's move on and look at adding player starts to our map.

Time for action – adding a player start

1. If you've been following the chapters so far, you may have noticed a lot of errors that look like the following:

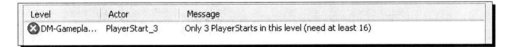

2. Unreal supports up to 16 players in Deathmatch, so we need to have at least 16 **PlayerStart** actors. Normally, your level will be big enough so that placing all of these spawn points will make sense and you may place some more, but it probably seems kind of silly right now. That's ok; we still want to place 16. You can place a new **PlayerStart** node by right-clicking on the ground, selecting **Add Actor**, and clicking on **Add PlayerStart**:

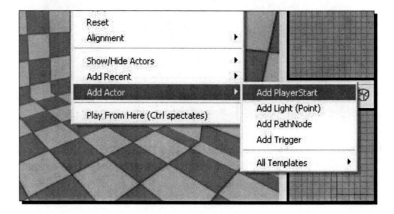

3. If you've already placed one, you can clone it around by *alt*+click+dragging on one of the move tool's handles. Do this until you have 16 nodes spread all over your level. Try to make sure they're at least 128 units apart:

Remember you can middle+click+drag in a 2D view to use the measure tool.

4. Also, see the little blue wireframe arrow pointing out of the nodes. That's the direction in which the player will be facing when he/she spawns. You may want to rotate some of your **PlayerStart** nodes so that they're facing in a sensible direction:

What just happened?

So, we know how to add player starts using the **Actors** tab in the content browser. Let's now test our map by playing it in the editor, and see what happens when we add bots to our map using the *Tab* key to bring up the in-game console.

Time for action – play in editor

1. We'll cover this in more detail in another tutorial, but you can test your map by clicking the **Play in Editor** button (the little black joystick at the top-right corner of the window):

2. If your map shows up black, or just generally isn't doing what you expect, you may have to hit **Build All** and try again:

3. Once you're up and running properly, press the *Tab* key to bring up the console, and type `addbots 1`. A bot should appear somewhere in your level:

You can, of course, add as many bots as you want with that command, up to 16.

What just happened?

So, we have added our player starts to the map and have now tested them within the editor using the in-game command *Tab*. You may or may not know, but the bots are all over the place at the moment; we will come to that later by adding something called **bot pathing**, which will pinpoint where the bots are allowed or not allowed to go in your map. For now, let's have a look at placing pickups in our level.

Time for action – placing pickups

So you can run around your level and shoot stuff, but without weapon pickups, health, and armor, the level feels kind of dull. We can get at all of the weapon pickups and a lot of other good stuff through the **Actor Class** browser.

1. Open up your generic browser and click on the tab labeled **Actor Classes** at the top of the window:

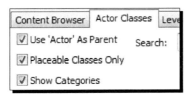

2. Finding pickups in the list is hard unless you know where to look. They're all hidden under the **Navigation** point. That's because, from a code standpoint, they're all based-off of the code that knows how to create paths. Open up **Navigation** point, then **Pickup Factory**, then **UTPickupFactory**. You'll start to see some of the things you're looking for, such as a **Weapon Pickup Factory**. You can open up subfolders to get at other object types, such as **Ammo**, **Armor**, **Health**, **Powerups**, and **Weapon Lockers**:

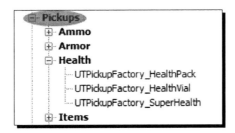

3. Select one of the bold items (say, **UTPickupFactory_HealthVial**):

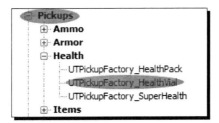

4. Now right-click in the world, and then click on **Add UTPickupFactory_HealthVial Here**:

5. As you'd expect, a health vial appears.

If you generate paths and run your map, you'll be able to pick up the health vial to heal yourself, and bots will pick it up as well.

What just happened?

So, we know how to place pickups into our map from the **Actors** tab in the content browser. So what's next? Guns, lots of guns. Let's now have a look at placing weapons in our map again using the **Actors** tab in the content browser. Remember that all weapons and inventory are located in the **Actors** tab.

Time for action – placing weapons

Most pickups, such as the health vial, just require you to place them in the world and you're good to go. But for weapon pickups and weapon lockers, you need to specify what kind of weapons will be available.

1. Place an **UTWeaponPickupFactory** in your level in the same way you placed the health vial. Make sure that the object is selected in the world, then click on **View | Actor Properties** or double-click on the object, or press *F4*.

2. Every object, even static meshes and brushes, have properties that you can set. There are lots of categories in the properties window, and most of those categories, such as **Display**, **Movement**, and **Object** are used by every type of actor. In most cases, you only care about the properties for the specific type of actor you're working on. In this case, we want to set the weapon pickup factory properties, so click on the **UTWeaponPickupFactory category**. It may already be open.

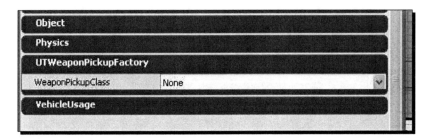

3. You can now pick what type of weapon you want by clicking on the word **None** to the right of **WeaponPickupClass** and choosing one of the weapon options, as shown in the following screenshot:

4. If you run the game, the weapon shows up, as shown in the following screenshot:

5. Weapon lockers are a little more complicated to configure. Add an **UTWeaponLocker_Content** to your level, the same way you added the **UTWeaponPickupFactory**. Open up its properties and open the **UTWeaponLocker** category.

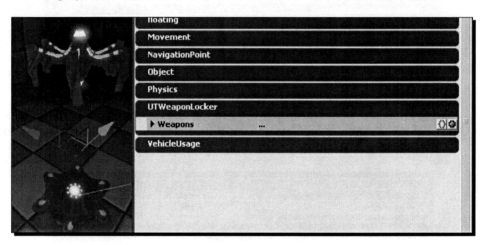

6. It looks like we can have a whole list of weapons, but right now there's nothing in the list. Click the little black arrow; you'll see that there's nothing. To add more weapons to the locker, click the little green dot on the right side of the window. You'll see that a new line appears underneath.

7. Open that up, and you can set the **WeaponClass**, just like you did earlier.

8. Clicking the green dot multiple times lets you add lots of weapons to the locker. Mouse over the other icons too, as they let you do some neat stuff, for example, they help you delete a weapon from the list:

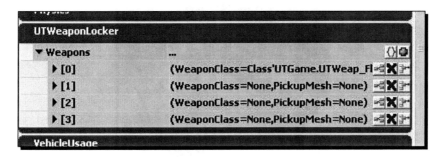

9. One final note about pickups. When you build paths, is you'll probably notice warnings, as shown in the following screenshot:

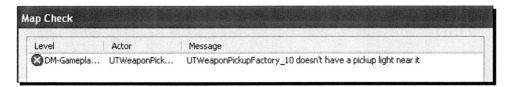

10. Don't even worry about figuring out what pickup lights are, or placing them manually. Just go to **Tools | Add Pickup Lights**:

11. Lights will automatically be created over every pickup. If you've moved or deleted a pickup, the old light will be updated properly.

What just happened?

So, now we have an arsenal of weapons to choose from in our map, but what else can we incorporate into our map? Why not jump pads. If you have more than one level in your map, it might be ideal to have a couple of jump pads floating around, so how do we do that?

Time for action – placing jump pads

Jump pads launch the player into the air, ultimately to come down at a specified location.

1. To create a jump pad, you need to place a jump pad base and then tell it where the player is supposed to land. But first, modify your level so that one of the rooms has a ledge or a platform that is big enough to run around on.

2. Placing a jump pad is the same as placing any pickup. It's in the **Actor Classes** browser under **Navigation** point. It's called **UTJumpPad**. Create one next to your ledge, about 128 units out.

3. Also place a navigation point on top of the ledge; the jump pad will eventually lead here:

4. We specify the jump pad's target in its properties window, similar to how we specified what weapon a weapon pickup will spawn.

Open up the jump pad's properties window, and open up the **UTJumpPad** category. Aha! There's a box labeled **Jump Target** and a few other controls, which I'll let you explore on your own, once the whole thing is hooked up.

What we need to do is plug our pathnode into the **Jump Target** box. We need to select the pathnode and then click on the little green arrow to the right of **Jump Target**, but selecting the pathnode would bring up its properties instead of the jump pad's properties. So, while you still have the jump pad selected, click on the lock icon in the top-left of the window. This locks the properties on the jump pad, no matter what you select.

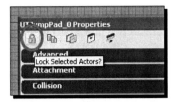

5. Now select the path node and click the green arrow next to the **Jump Target** property; the path node name should fill in.

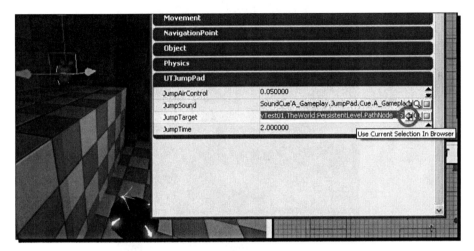

6. Now build paths. With any luck, you'll see a curved line going from the jump pad to the path node. If you're like me though, you got an error saying the jump can't be made.

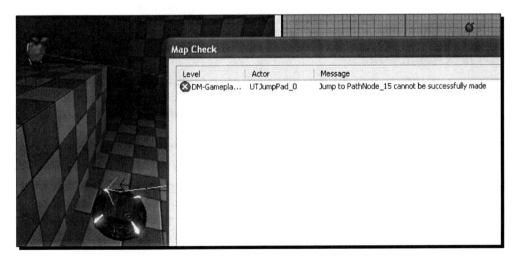

7. In my case, my ceiling was too low. I raised it and the jump pad works fine now. You might also run into problems if the jump pad is too close to the ledge, or if the path node is too far from the edge of the ledge.

What just happened?

So now we have jump pads in our map, which will let us navigate easier around levels, but is there anything else that we can do with our map? What if we want teleporter or vehicles? How do we go about adding them to our map? I'm going to show you how.

Time for action – adding other game object types

Now that you know how to create pickups and jump pads, you should be able to figure out any other gameplay object type. I'll give a rough overview of some of the common ones here, without going into full detail. This section is meant to be more of a reference guide, but if you want to add some of these object types to your level now, it'll be a good practice.

Let us begin with the **teleporter**.

A teleporter is something that transfers matter from one point to another, more or less instantaneously.

1. To place a teleporter pad, select **Navigation | Teleporter | UTTeleporter** and place one in your level. You'll also need an exit point for your teleporter. You can create another **UTTeleporter**, which will spawn with a base in the level.

2. Under the **Teleporter** properties, there's a field called **URL**. This is the **Tag** of the teleporter destination. Select the teleport destination, bring up its properties, and open up **object**. In the **Tag** field, give it a name like `TeleDest01`. Go back to your original teleporter, and fill in the destination's **Tag** under **URL**:

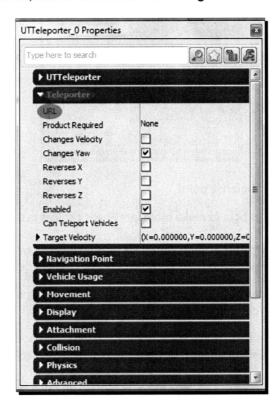

3. You can also easily make the teleporter two-way, by giving both a unique tag and setting each **UTTeleporter URL** to the other. You can even make a chain or loop of teleporters that all go to each other in order:

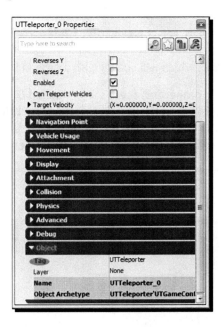

Next, let us look at the **UTDefense point**.

The UTDefense point helps bots to make more intelligent choices in a CTF or Warfare game.

1. Place UTDefense points around your flags or power cores, or any place where defense is important.

2. Point the **DefendedObjective** parameter at the specific flag or power node that you want the bots to defend.

3. You can also type a name in the **DefenseGroup** field, and bots in **defend** mode will move between defend nodes that have a matching **DefenseGroup** name.

There are a few other parameters as well, but they should be self-explanatory.

Next, let us look at the **UTTranslocatorDest**.

Building paths will automatically create some translocator jump paths, but sometimes you'll want to force them to a specific location to a power-up on a high ledge.

1. Create an **UTTranslocatorDest** where you want the translocator to land. In the properties, open up the **UTTranslocatorDest**.

2. You can now click the green button to add multiple start point slots, and then connect them to path node using the **Point** parameter, just like you did with the **Jump Target** on the jump pad.

Next, let us look at the **Lift** (**LiftCenter/LiftExit**)

Basically, the lift **pad** is an InterpActor controlled by a matinee sequence, so that it moves up and down on a timer, or it could be triggered through Kismet to move when the player steps on it. A **LiftCenter** is a part of the path network that lets bots actually use your lift. It's attached to the InterpActor (under the **LiftCenter** properties, **Attachment | Base**). Attaching the **LiftCenter** makes it follow the InterpActor's movement. **LiftExits** are the other important part of the path network. They have a **MyLiftCenter** variable, which you need to point at the **LiftCenter**:

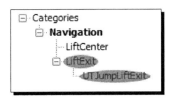

Next, let us look at the **Vehicles**.

Vehicles are very easy to add to a map.

1. Go into the **Actor Classes** window and open up **Vehicles**. Select the vehicle type you want, right-click and add it to the level.

   ❑ In a VCTF or War game, the vehicle's team will automatically be determined by who owns the objective node it's closest to. So, if it's placed closest to the blue team's flag, it'll belong to the blue team.

   ❑ In a Deathmatch game, any bot will attempt to use the vehicle.

   Of course, you need to make sure your level has spaces wide enough for the vehicle to pass through.

2. If you want to place a vehicle boost pad, select **UTVehicleBoostPad** from the main **Actor Classes** menu (not under **Navigation** point) and add it to the level like normal. A semi-transparent box with a scrolling texture will appear. You can non-uniformly scale it to get it to fit the area you need.

   Remember to make it extra tall if you want it to affect flying vehicles.

3. Under the object's properties, you can control which types of vehicles are affected by it (like limiting it to the hover board). You can also control how much power the boost has.

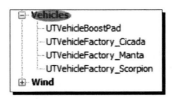

Next, let us look at the **Capture the Flag** maps.

CTF maps are easy to create. There are only a few things that differentiate them from Deathmatch maps.

1. Name the file **CTF-[mapname]** for a standard Capture the Flag map, or name it **VCTF** for Vehicle Capture the Flag.

2. Add a flag base for each team. Find them in the **Actor Classes** browser under **NavigationPoint | Objective | UTGameObjective | UTCTFBase | UTCTFBase_ Content**. Add them like you would add any other gameplay object.

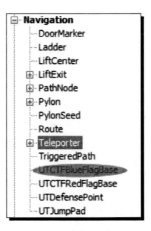

3. You also need to place a special kind of player start node and tag it with the team that will spawn from it. You can place a **Team PlayerStart** node, by selecting **UTTeamPlayerStart** in the **ActorClasses** browser under **Common | PlayerStart | UDKTeamPlayerStart | UTTeamPlayerStart**.

4. Place one in the world, open up its properties, and open up the **UTTeamPlayerStart** category. Set the **TeamNumber** field to 0 for the red team and 1 for the blue team.

5. You may also want to set up some **UTDefensePoints**, as described in the previous section.

What just happened?

So these are the gameplay elements thrown into your map player starts, pick-ups, weapon placing, jump pads, lifts, teleporter, vehicles, and flags along with testing of your map in-game. We can now look at controlling where the bots are allowed to go and where not to go by adding bot pathing around our map.

Have a go hero – adding music to your map

It is really essential to add music to the level. Music nowadays is also responsible for certain gameplay sounds, such as the tune played when someone captures the flag, so it is really essential that you set it up, otherwise the game would sound very dull.

Music isn't just a single track anymore in UDK. You actually assign about ten sound samples to the level, each for other circumstances. These ten or so samples are held by a **music arrangement** asset. It is the music arrangement that you assign to a level, and not the individual tracks.

1. Go to the generic browser, and open the package A_Music_Arrangements.upk found in the folder **UDK version | UTGame | Content | UT3 | Sounds | Music**.

2. Pick the one you like most, and while having it selected in the generic browser, go to the top menu of the editor **View | World Properties**.

3. Extend **World Info** in the window that pops up, and add an item to **My MapInfo** using the blue arrow on the right.

4. Enter the desired music set to the **MapMusicInfo** property.

Bot pathing

I've done bot pathing before for my maps, and after watching some tutorial videos, it's not really that hard. I'll try to explain it as simply as possible.

Time for action – adding path nodes

Bots are stupid. All they know to do is point at the nearest target and shoot, or run for the nearest pickup that's in sight. They're great at getting to things they can see. But how do they get from room to room? If their health is low, how do they find their way to a health pickup? Well, Unreal generates a path network that connects everything in your level. That way, if a bot has no one to shoot, or is low on health, they know how to run through hallways to different rooms where there are goodies for them to pick up.

1. To start, click on the **Build Paths** button at the top of the screen:

2. Paths are automatically generated, connecting every player start in the level. You can view your path network by clicking on the black arrow that's at the top of a viewport and clicking on **Paths**, or you can just press the hotkey *P*.

3. Any player starts that are in view of each other should now have a line connecting them.

4. But what do we do in a situation where **PlayerStart** nodes can't see each other? We definitely don't want to move the **PlayerStart**, or add more.

5. Unreal has an actor called a **PathNode**, which does exactly what we want—we can place it in the hallway, and Unreal will connect our rooms together. Right-click on the floor, then select **Add Actor | Add PathNode**, or better yet use the shortcut— hold down the key and click on the floor:

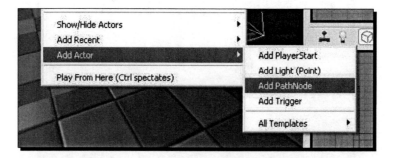

6. An apple icon appears. Click the **Build Paths** button and you should see some more connections. You may have to move the **PathMode** around and rebuild paths to get it to connect up, or you may need to add more than one **PathNode**.

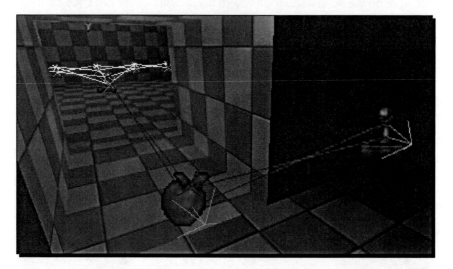

7. Add a few **PathNodes** to your map now and make sure every room is connected by paths. Run the game and add a few bots, and you'll see they're now able to traverse the whole space.

What just happened?

So we know how bot pathing works and how to place path nodes around the map. This will not only show the bots how to navigate around certain areas of your map, but also show them where they cannot go.

Pop quiz

What are the four different types of naming convention?

Summary

We learned a lot in this chapter about:

- Naming the different types of map convention
- Adding a player start to our map
- Placing pickups in our map
- Placing weapons in our map
- Placing jump pads in our map
- Adding other game objective types to our map
- Placing path nodes in our map

So that's how you add gameplay elements such as player starts, special pickups, weapons, jump pads, and other gameplay elements such as teleporter and vehicles. We also have learnt how to use path nodes to create a path where the bots will navigate around our map. In the next chapter, we will be looking at basic Kismet scripting.

8
Complex Event Sequences

Upon first glance, a blank Kismet page can be quite daunting. After some practice, you'll find yourself eager to fill it. Kismet is where the user can create movers, script events, turn particles on and off, perhaps even change some AI, and even more. Kismet can be thought of as a **Graphical User Interface** *(***GUI***) that brings code accessibility to those who want to manipulate the engine and create something new. Friendly little circles and rectangles allow the user to construct simple or complex sequences to enhance the game's impact on the player.*

In this chapter we shall be looking at the following:

◆ A simple sequence
◆ Basic UIScene
◆ Basic cut scene

So let's begin...

Time for action – a simple sequence

The simple sequence is going to be a single message that fires off when the level starts. I'm assuming that my dear reader will know how to set up a simple piece of BSP and add a light and PlayerStart to it (and rebuild). This needs to be done so that the player can survive long enough to see the message.

1. Anywhere in the Kismet browser, right-click | **New Event** | **Level Startup**:

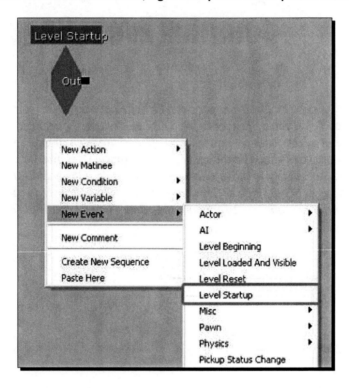

2. Then right-click | **New Action** | **Misc** | **Log**:

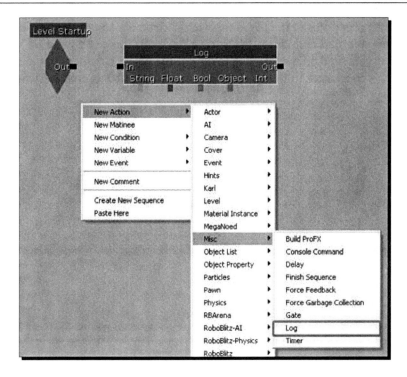

3. Link them together by making a line between the **Out** of the **Level Startup** and the **In** of the **Log**:

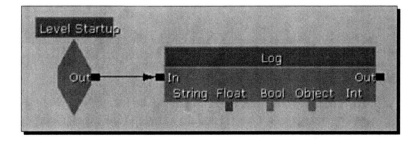

4. Alter the properties of the **Log**. Simply left-click on the **Log** to select it. Add an **Obj Comment** (object comment), in this case **Tutorial!**. Then, to ensure we know that the **Log** gets fired off, we're going to output the object comment to the screen by adding a checkmark to the box to the right of **bOutputObjCommentToScreen**:

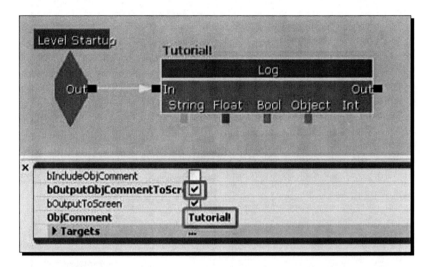

And that's about it. When the map is launched, the player will spawn and a **Tutorial!** will appear in text at the bottom left of the screen.

If object comments and **Logs** don't work, your engine may be set to disable these **debug** messages in game. To fix this, you may need to try several things.

 The following involves changing .ini files for the games. This can cause things to go horribly awry in some cases, so back up the files first.

5. Find your `DefaultEngine.ini` file. This file will be located at different places for different engines/games. Open it and do a search for Kismet. One of the first results will be `bOnScreenKismetWarnings=FALSE`. You'll need to change this to `bOnScreenKismetWarnings=TRUE`. Save the .ini and see if it works.

6. If this does not work, after the `bOnScreenKismetWarnings=FALSE` line add this line: `bEnableKismetLogging=TRUE`.

7. This may work, but is generally not recommended since it may very well be a **cooked** file depending on the game. Look for the game-specific `xxxengine.ini` where xxx is the game, and enable the same two settings there.

8. If it still does not work, you'll need to rely only on logs while in **Play In Editor** (**PIE**) mode and not the game itself. You can add logs or instructions below, however, you'll only be able to view them in the generic browser's **Log** tab, and only if you set the `bIncludeObjComment` boolean to `true`. The text will appear in the generic browser's **Log**, but not on the screen.

9. If even this does not work, then there's one route left. Instead of using a log, grab an emitter and place it where you can see it. Use a toggle action to turn it on when you would want the log to go off. Thus, if the emitter goes off, you'll know that portion is working. Remember to turn off the `AutoActivate` property in the emitter.

What just happened?

So we know how to create a single message sequence using simple basic kismet scripting, which will be triggered off when the player starts the level. Let's take this further by looking at basic UIScenes and creating a clip, which will run for 5 seconds just before the match begins.

Have a go hero – preview screenshot

Why not have a go hero at creating a preview screenshot for your level? Take a screenshot of your level and crop/resize it to a resolution of 512 pixels width, 256 pixels high. Save it as a `TGA` file, preferably name it `Screenshot`, and import it into the package of your level.

Time for action – basic UIScene

1. Start by creating a new UIScene, somewhere in the generic browser. So make a new package add it to an existing package, or embed it into your level (by naming the package exactly the same as your level). Whatever you pick, right-click in that package and pick **New UIScene**:

New MaterialInstanceTimeVarying(WIP)
New MultiFont Imported From TrueType
New ParticleSystem
New Physical Material
New Post Process Effect
New RenderToTexture
New RenderToTextureCube
New SoundCue
New SoundNodeWaveTTS
New SpeechRecogniser
New TerrainLayerSetup
New TerrainMaterial
New UIScene
New UT Map Music

2. The UIScene editor should open automatically. If it does not, simply double-click the UIScene in the generic browser.

The UIScene editor is navigated much like the others Sub editors. Left or right mouse pans the view. Holding both zooms in and out. Zoom out until you see the blue frame. This is the edge of the screen, so whatever you do, make sure it is inside this frame.

3. Right-click somewhere in an empty space and pick the **Place Widget** and then **Label** at the top of the list. A label now shows up at the top-left of the screen. Drag it somewhere else holding the *Ctrl* key and dragging the mouse. Scale it up if you want:

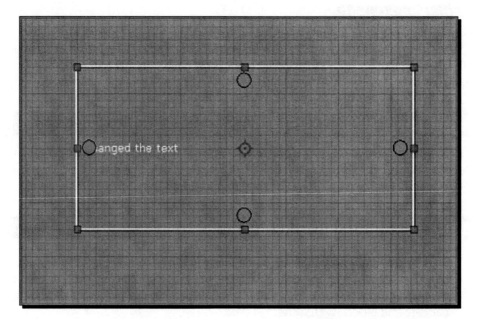

4. On the right side is a **Properties** section. If you do not see this section, go to the top menu and click **Window | Properties**. In **Properties**, go to **Data | DataSource | MarkupString**. This is the text displayed, so change this to whatever you want:

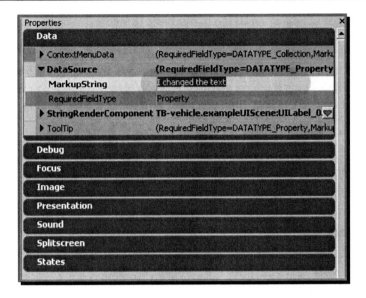

5. Further down below in **Data**, there is the **StringRenderComponent**. In there is
StyleOverride. This bit holds a few interesting properties that allow you to quickly
alter the appearance of the text. In my example, I changed the color, assigned a
different (and higher quality) font, and scaled it up:

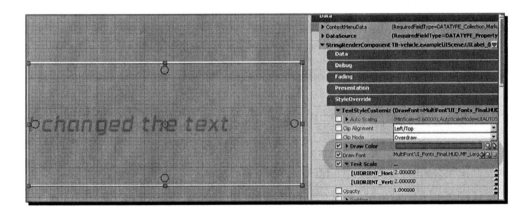

In UT3, fonts can be found in the packages `UI_Fonts` and `UI_Fonts_Final`. If
you want to display big text, make sure you pick a high quality and large font. Unlike
most other programs, not every font can be scaled up to whatever size you want.
The fonts are actually images, so the quality depends on the resolution of the image.
Therefore, if you want big text you need a high resolution font. So choose wisely.

Let's now have a look at adding an image to our basic UIScene.

1. Right-click again somewhere in an empty space, place a widget, and go for image this time, also near the top of the list. Again, move and expand the image frame it creates. Notice how it covers up the text if you place over it. If you want the image to appear behind the text, then you must give the text a higher priority.

2. Right-click the image | **Reorder Widget** | **Move to Bottom**:

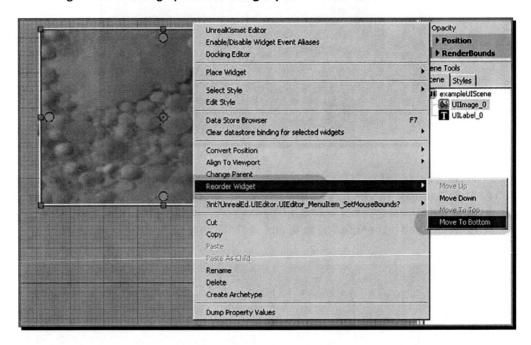

3. Next, assign an actual image to the frame. Select the image frame and in its properties, navigate to **Image** | **ImageComponent** | **StyleOverride** | **ImageRef**. Add a texture here:

   And note that it must be a texture, not a material.

   I applied a screenshot of the game and my test scene appears as shown in the following screenshot:

Let's now have a look at docking and how we can make our image and text cover the entire screen.

4. Next up is docking. At the top left of the **UIScene Editor**, you can see a drop-down menu with resolutions. Change this to some other number and see what happens to your text and image. Try a very low resolutions, such as 640×480. It probably doesn't look all that nice on all these resolutions. Unless what you made is very small, it likely goes out of the blue frame on low resolutions, and that is really bad.

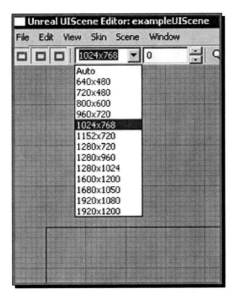

You need to tell the editor to correctly scale and move the elements inside the UIScene along with the resolution that was set.

5. Select either the text or the image, and notice the big four orange dots in the middle of each side. These allow you to hook up that side to some other element and basically lock it.

   Select one of these and start dragging. Notice how red dots appear on the blue frame. Drag it to these to make it connect. Connect all sides to the corresponding sides of the blue frame.

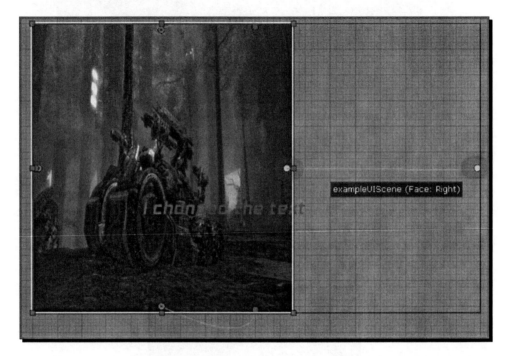

   This will make your image or your text cover the entire screen. Scale the resolution up or down and notice how the text and/or the image now do correctly scale along.

6. Next we are going to make sure that it doesn't cover the entire screen, but has some empty space around it. Right-click the image or the text, dependent what you linked to the blue frame, and open the **Docking Editor**:

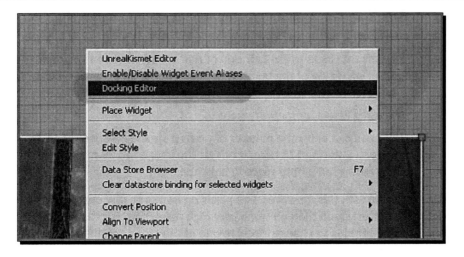

7. This little sub-sub editor gives you some more control over how elements are locked together:

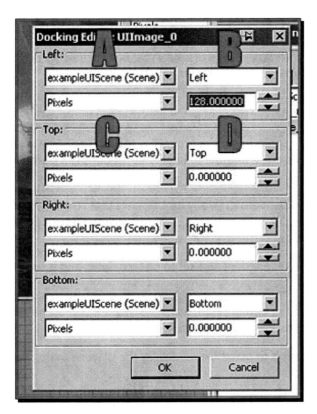

- ◆ **A**: The **Left** side locks to **exampleUIScene**, which is the blue frame. The blue frame has the name that you gave to the UIScene in the generic browser.
- ◆ **B**: My **Left** side locks to the **Left** side of that blue frame. So this property identifies what side of the target it should connect to; usually you want to select the same side here.
- ◆ **C**: It is using **Pixels** for measurement.
- ◆ **D**: Here you can enter the number of pixels it should be offsetted to, from that edge. Upon entering **128** here, it offsets the image to 128 pixels from the blue frame, creating an empty space in between.

Do be careful with this, however. 128 pixels on 640×480 obviously covers a whole lot more of the screen than on some very high resolution. For that reason, it is usually a better idea to change **Pixels** to one of the other options given, such as **Percentage of Screen**.

> You can also enter negative numbers, if you want, to offset it into the other direction. If you would have entered **128** pixels on the right side, it would offset the element away from the screen. The center of the scene is in the middle of the screen, so if you want to bring something away from the edge on the left side, you would need +128, but -128 on the right side. The same goes for top and bottom.

Let's now look at the different types of properties that can improve our UIScene.

Click onto some empty space to get the properties section to display the main properties of the entire UIScene. In there, a number of interesting options can be found, which are listed as follows:

- ◆ **Disable World Rendering**: Handy for UIScenes that cover the entire screen.
- ◆ **bDisplayCursor**: To display the mouse cursor or not. By default it's set to on, which is not a good thing to have for cut scene text, for example.
- ◆ **bPauseGameWhileActive**: Also set to on by default, and is usually not really desirable.

The final part is to add the Kismet script, which will make our UIScene appear at the start of the level and decide how long it will appear for.

Finally, the last thing left is to make Kismet display the UIScene during the game.

1. Open Kismet and add **New Event | Level Startup**. Next, **New Action | UI**, and add both **Open Scene** and **Close Scene**. It would also be a good idea to add a **Delay** in between, found in **New Action | Misc | Delay**.

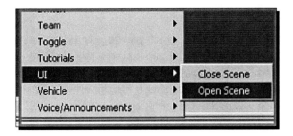

2. Hook it up as shown in the screenshot, and be sure to fill in the UIScene you made in both the **Open Scene** and **Close Scene** properties, otherwise it will not work.

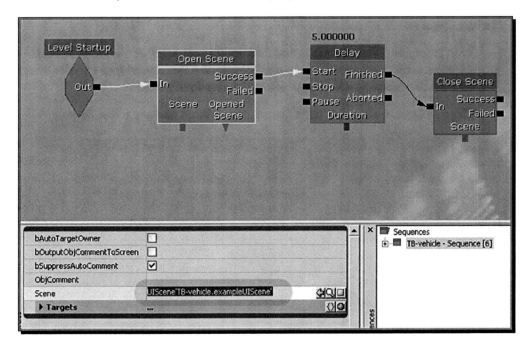

3. Upon starting the level, this set up will display your scene for five seconds and then close it again. If you want to display multiply scenes, continue adding **Open Scene** and **Close Scene** nodes.

What just happened?

So we have just created a basic UIScene, which will appear as soon as we start our level in-game and will last for 5 seconds before the game starts. We know to create the scene from scratch, which will be used, followed by adding an image, and will appear in the UI scene. We also know how to dock the UIScene so that it fits the entire screen, and finally adding the kismet scripting, which will make the scene appear at the start of a match and how it will stay up for before it disappears. Let's now have a look at creating a basic cut scene that utilizes two cameras, fades in and out, and triggers an event along the way.

Time for action – basic cut scene

The first Camera:

1. Go to the **Actor Classes** browser, and find the **Camera Actor** at the top of the list. Place this actor in your level on the desired location. It is a good idea to point it into the right direction already, though you could also do this later.

2. Once the **Camera Actor** has been placed, open Kismet and add a **Matinee**:

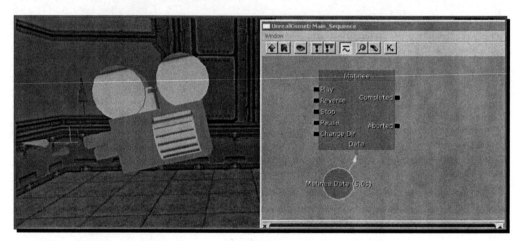

3. Open that **Matinee** by double-clicking it. Make sure the **Camera Actor** is selected in the viewport when you do this.

4. Right-click the dark gray space and pick **Add New Director Group**:

5. Now right-click the dark gray space again and pick **Add New Camera Group**. You now have two items in **Matinee**:

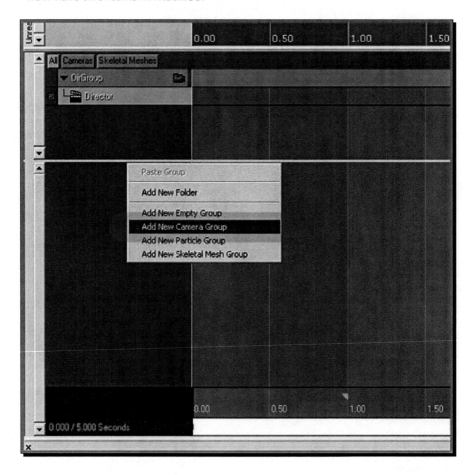

6. The camera group controls the camera. Each camera will have its own group, the director controls when which camera is active. So the first thing we should do is tell the director to start using your single camera. To do this, make sure the timeline is currently set at 0.0 (which is the case by default), click on **Director**, so it turns orange, and then click the **Add Key** button at the top left.

It then pops up a box that asks you what to cut to; select your camera group:

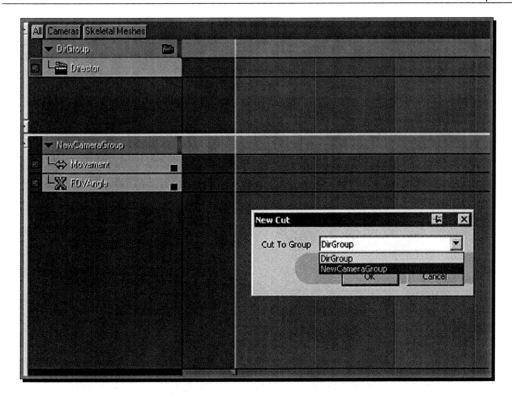

7. Next, we want to animate the camera itself. Click on **Movement**, which is part of your camera group, and then click the **Add Key** button once more, to add a first position/key to the timeline.

    Matinee should now preview the position and angle of the camera in your viewport. If it does not cut to the camera in your viewport, it may help to close matinee and open it again. Alternatively, you can mess with the little camera button on the right of **Director Group**, which actually toggles viewport camera previewing on and off.

8. When **Matinee** previews your camera in the viewport, it will also record your moves in it. This way you can position cameras by simply adding a key, and then fly or rotate the camera how you want in the viewport, and it will remember this. It will, however, not remember the path you took to fly to that location, but only the final position.

And that is what we are going to do. So, make sure the viewport previews the camera and add another key to the camera group. Make sure you have **Movement** selected in the camera group; put the timeline on some other time, and hit the **Add Key** button again:

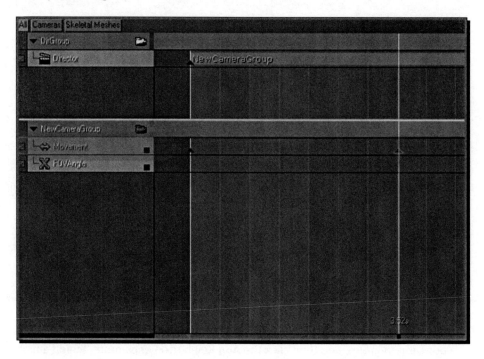

9. Without doing anything else, fly the camera in the viewport to where you want it to go (while keeping matinee open), when you are done, put the timeline in **Matinee** back to 0.0, and hit Play. The cut scene should now preview in the viewport.

10. Close **Matinee**, and in Kismet add **New Event | Level Startup**, and connect it to play the **Matinee**.

You now have a very basic cut scene that starts as soon as the level starts.

The second Camera:

1. Go to the **Actor Classes** browser again and add a second camera actor. Continue by opening Kismet and then **Matinee** again, and add a **NewCameraGroup** below your first one.

2. Then, select the **Director** and put the timeline to when you want the **Director** to switch to the second camera. Add a key and be sure to select the second camera, grouping the menu that pops up:

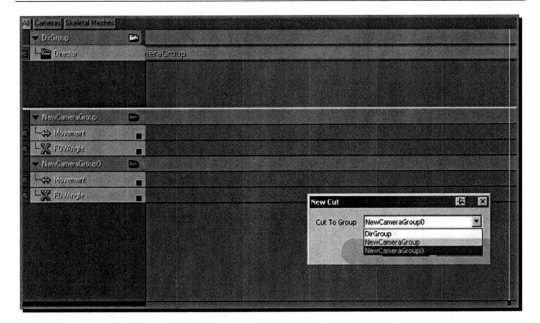

3. Animate this camera as well, and you are done!

You now have a basic cut scene that makes use of two different cameras.

More on Cameras:

1. If the camera rotates strangely while flying around, select the **Movement** track of that camera in **Matinee** and have a look at the properties that show up at the bottom of the window. Enable **bUseQuatInterpolation**.

2. There are some other interesting properties as well. The ones I personally use most are `LinCurveTension` and `AngCurveTension`. They control how smooth the camera flies through the world. A value of `1.00000` would create very blocky yet precise movement, whereas the default value of `0.000000` smooths the movement out, but that may also cause the camera to fly through geometry every now and then.

3. As those two settings still offer only limited control over how the camera moves, it's well recommended to manually tweak the paths of your cameras. To view the paths, disable **Camera Previewing** in the viewport by clicking that little (yellow) camera on the right of the **Director Group**.

4. You should now see colored lines with little dots on. This is the path it follows. Now, if you click on a key in **Matinee**, you will see that two white lines show up, one on either side of the position. These control the curves:

5. Click on the little square at the end of one of these lines and drag it. Notice how the entire line changes. You can also hold both mouse buttons to drag it around, as that gives more freedom of movement. It is a bit cumbersome to tweak the paths like this, but if done right, it will greatly improve the quality of your cut scene.

6. Lastly, in the regular properties of your **Camera Actor** itself (regular properties being the *F4* one), you are able to configure the **AspectRatio** and the **Field Of View** in the section **CameraActor**. If you disable **bConstrainAspectRatio**, it will not render these black borders. These black borders only show up when the ratio of the screen does not match the **AspectRatio** set there. And as you can see, you are also able to change the post process settings here, on a per camera basis.

Fading and events:

7. Adding a fade in and out is fairly easy. In **Matinee**, right-click **DirGroup** and pick **Add New Fade Track**:

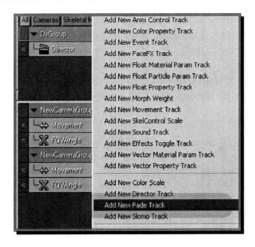

8. Now add keys where you want a fade to start and where it should end. If we want to have a fade in and out, we would thus have to have 4 keys.

Add a key at **0.0**, a key at **1.0**, and a key at **1.00** second before the end of your cuts cene, and finally the last key at the very end of your cut scene.

9. Then click the tiny black square on the right of fade.

This adds the fade track to the curve editor at the top of the window.

10. In the curve editor, you are going to create the curves that control the fading. You should now see a horizontal line in that window, with four squares, corresponding the locations of your keys. Right-click the first square, and select **Set Value**; enter 1.0:

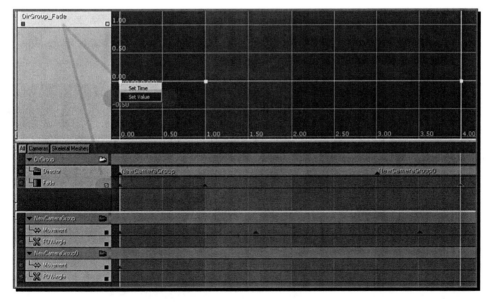

1.0 is black or thus fully faded out. **0.00** means no fade at all. You thus want the first and the last key to be **1.0**, and the ones in between **0.00**. Now set the last square to **1.0** as well.

11. Your curve may be going below **0.00** in the middle, and thus will be negative. To fix this, select the second square and hit the button with the diagonal line at the top:

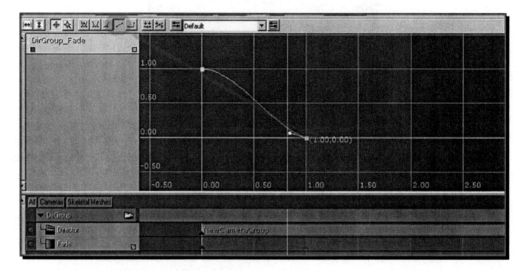

You are now done with the fading part.

If you want to trigger an external event during the cut scene, you can add an event track. On this event track, every key represents an event that can trigger something else in Kismet.

12. To add one, right-click **DirGroup** again, and pick **New Event Track** this time. Now add a key for it somewhere and enter the name:

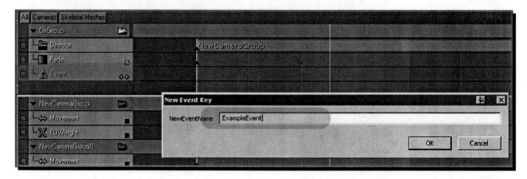

13. Exit **Matinee** and you should see that the event showed up on the **Matinee** node in Kismet. You can now hook that one up to whatever you want; in my case it is healing the **Player**:

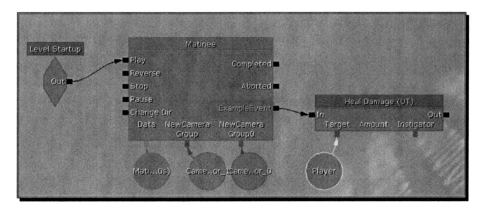

What just happened?

So we know how to create a basic cut scene with two different cameras, an event triggered along the way, and a fade in and out. You now have basic knowledge of the editor and **Matinee** browsers.

Summary

We learned a lot in this chapter. Specifically, we covered the following:

◆ How to create a simple text sequence that will appear at the beginning of the level

◆ How to create a basic UIScene with an image and text that will appear before the match begins

◆ How to create a basic cut scene with two different cameras, an event triggered along the way, and a fade in and out

So we have a basic understanding of complex event sequences, like creating text that appears at the beginning of a player spawn, or creating a UIScene, which displays images and text before the game commences. UIScene is a sub editor that is responsible for everything to do with the interface, all menus, the HUD, text displayed during the game, and so on. In the final chapter, we will be looking at materials and how to create our own materials.

9
Materials

This chapter will explain the basics of creating a material. We'll build some basic (but extremely useful) materials from scratch, and in the process learn how the material editor works.

In this chapter we shall be looking at the following topics:

- ◆ Creating a new material
- ◆ Adding textures to a material
- ◆ Creating a shiny metal surface
- ◆ Adding a normal map
- ◆ Seeing your material in the world
- ◆ Giving a perfect texture to your material
- ◆ Color specular highlight
- ◆ Adding a tint to the diffuse color
- ◆ Making your material easy to read

So let's begin...

What is a material?

A material, in essence, is a small computer program that describes how a surface looks. There's a lot we can do with our surfaces. Look around you; the world isn't just covered with flat paint.

Effects are easy to achieve with the Unreal material system, for instance, here's the material for a metal barrel. You can see in the preview on the left that it has a base color, shiny highlights, and ridges and bumps that bring out details in the surface. The node network in the middle is what describes how the surface looks, and that's what you're going to learn to build.

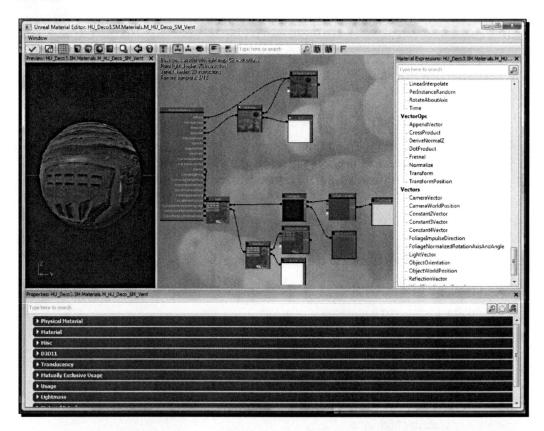

Time for action – creating a new material

Before you create a new material you'll need a place to test it.

1. Create a new level that's a simple BSP room with a light in it, build lighting, and save it as DM-MaterialTest.udk.

2. Open the generic browser, right-click in the blank gray space of the browser window to the right, and select **New Material**. Name your new material `BasicMaterial` and fill in a package name (either create a new package or fill in an existing one). Hit **OK**.

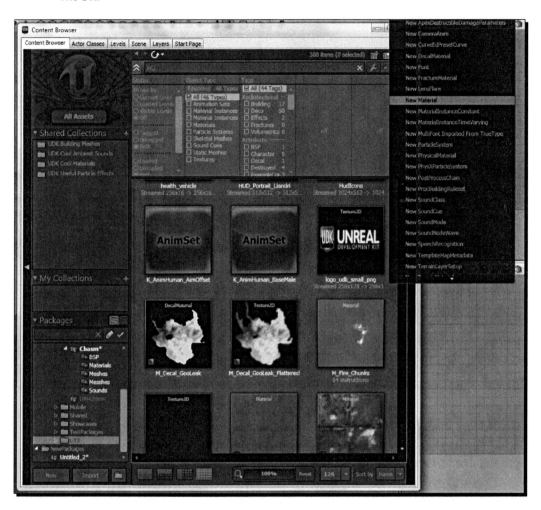

3. The material editor opens up. We haven't hooked up any nodes yet, so our material preview on the left is black. Let's fix that.

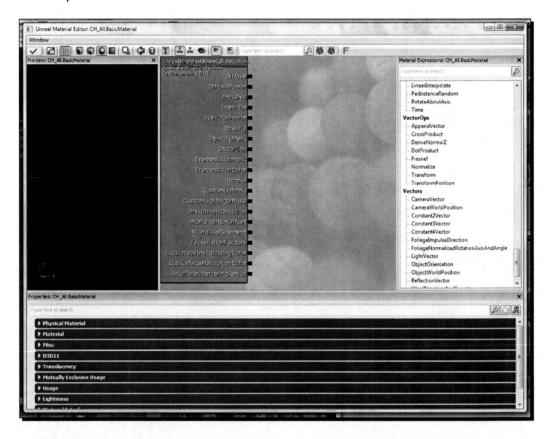

What just happened?

So, we have everything set up to create our first material. Let's start by finding a texture and applying that texture to our material.

Time for action – adding textures to a material

Practically every material you see in UDK gets its look from texture maps. Let's add one now.

1. Leave your **Material Editor** window open and switch to the generic browser.

2. Find the package labeled **HU_Deco**, right-click, and fully load it. Look for a texture labeled **M_HU_Deco_SM_Vent**. Look for it alphabetically, or you can filter by `type` to make your job easier.

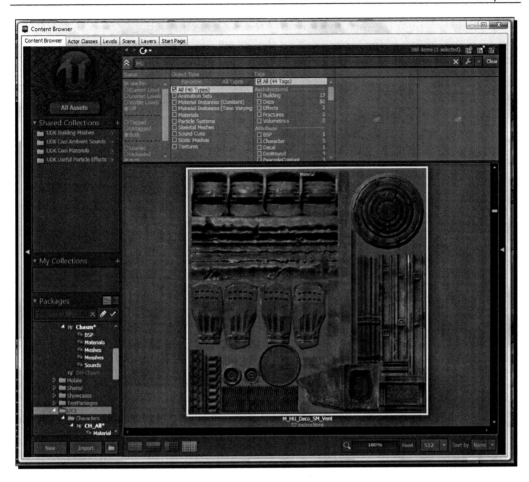

3. Select the texture and switch back to your material editor. What we want to do is create a node representing the texture. In the **Material Expressions** list on the right, scroll down until you see **Texture Sample**. Select it, then click-drag it into the gray viewport to the left, and a **Texture Sample** node should appear. If the node turns out black, you may not have had the texture selected in the generic browser. Delete it and try again.

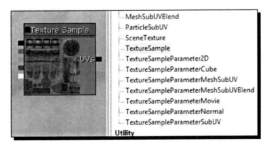

4. Now let's hook the texture node up so that it shows up on the surface. The black dot at the top-left of the texture node is the output. If you click-and-drag on that dot, a line will appear; drag a line to the **Diffuse** input of the big box to the left.

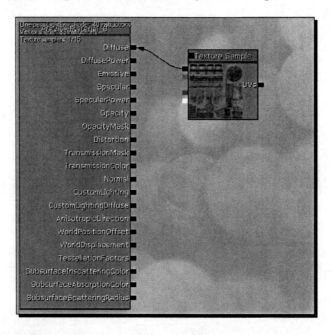

5. The line connects, and you should see a preview of your material on the left. **Diffuse** is the input that allows a texture to display on a surface. It's the basis for just about every material.

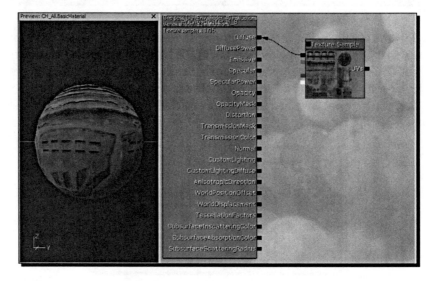

6. If you need to, you can move your **Texture Sample** node around by *ctrl*+click+dragging it. Give this a try now.

What just happened?

So, we have now created our first textured material, but at the moment it is looking pretty basic. So what can we do to make our material stand out more? I will now explain some steps to make your material realistic and stand out when used in your environment. Let's start by adding a shiny surface to our material.

Time for action – creating a shiny metal surface

This texture is supposed to represent a metal surface, so let's make the material shiny. There are a couple ways to do it, but let's use this opportunity to learn about a new node type—a **Constant**.

1. Find the word **Constant** in the **Material Expressions** list, and drag it into the editor viewport.

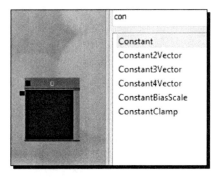

2. Connect the new **Constant** node to the **Specular** rendering terminology for shininess input on the left.

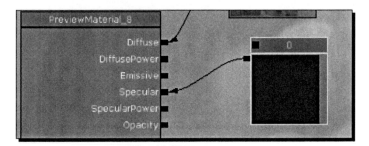

3. It didn't seem to have any effect. Right now, the constant has a value of 0, which means no specularity. Select the constant, and then at the bottom of the window, in the properties window, you'll see it has an **R** value of **0.000000**. Change it to 2.000000:

Type here to search	
R	2.000000
Desc	

4. Rotate the **Preview** cube around and you'll see that now it's much shinier.

Preview: CH_All.BasicMaterial

What just happened?

So, as you can see, we have applied **Specular** map to our material, which will give the texture a glossy finish, but as you can see in the previous image, it still doesn't look great. So what can we do to improve the quality of the specular map? We will now add a normal map, which will increase the divine characteristics of our texture. Normal mapping is used to bring the best out of your materials, which will make your environment look sharper and more atmospheric.

Time for action – adding a normal map

Right now, lighting affects the surface as if it were completely flat. We can add a normal map to make the material appear to have depth. You've probably noticed that for almost every diffuse texture, there's a pale blue texture with similar sorts of details. Those are normal maps.

1. Go back to the generic browser and search for **T_HU_Deco_SM_Vent_N**.

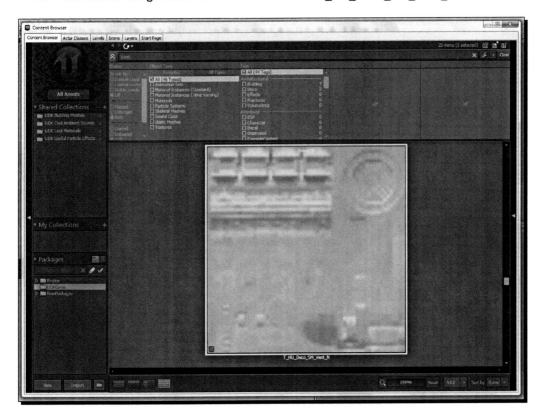

2. Select it, go back to your **Material Editor**, and drag another **Texture Sample** node into the editor. Hook it up to the **Normal** input of the box on the left.

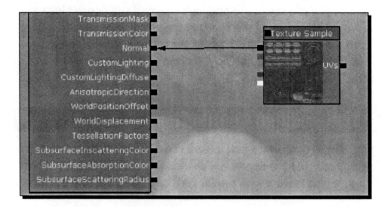

3. Now there's a lot more depth to the lighting and reflections.

4. Your node network should now look as shown in the following screenshot:

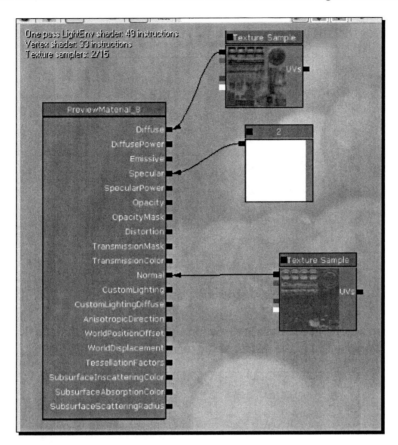

What just happened?

So, we have now added a normal map to our material, and as you can see from the images, it stands out a lot more than without the normal map. So what does it look like when we import it into our world; why not have a look. Let's now go ahead and apply the material to our map, and see what the results are.

Time for action – seeing your material in the world

1. You'll see that the material's thumbnail in the generic browser has updated.

2. You can apply it to a surface in the world—you can see here that the floor is reflecting the light in the middle of the room.

What just happened?

As you can see from the image above, this is what the material will look like when imported into our level, but it still doesn't look like metal; so how can we improve this? Let's go ahead and add some more maps to create the perfect material.

Time for action – giving a perfect texture to your material

1. So, as you can see from the image above, the material really doesn't look like metal. It's too bright for one thing, but it's also too uniformly shiny. The diffuse texture has lots of darker rusty areas that shouldn't be as shiny. You can hook the diffuse texture sample directly into the **Specular** input, and the color of the texture will control the specularity. Do that now.

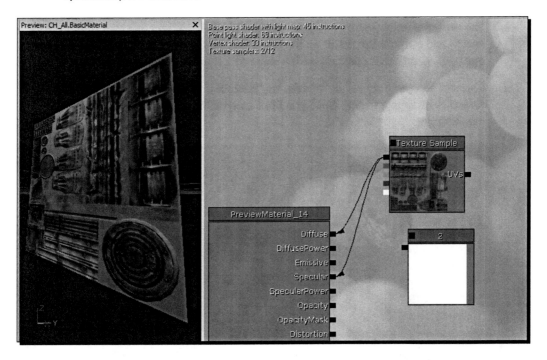

The highlight definitely looks better, but now it's probably too subtle. Let's look at how to brighten it up.

We can multiply the colors in the texture by a larger value so that they appear brighter.

2. Find a **Multiply** node in the **Material Expressions** list and drag it into the window.

The **Material** node (as you'd expect) multiplies two numbers together (the inputs **A** and **B**) and outputs the result on the left. What do we want for inputs? How about our texture, and that constant with a value of 2 that we created earlier?

3. Connect up your network as follows. You may have to rearrange the nodes (by *Ctrl*+click+dragging them). Once you hook everything up, you'll see the **Specular** highlight gets twice as bright.

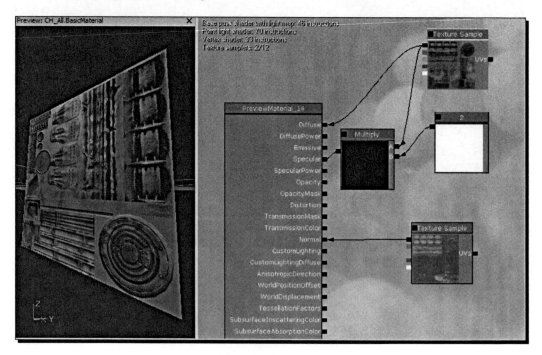

You can, of course, make it even brighter by selecting the **Constant** node and typing in a larger number. Change the value to 5.

4. Now, let's look at one more way to change the specularity of the material. Click on the **Sphere** icon at the top of the window; this changes the preview mesh from a cube to a sphere.

5. As you can see from the image below, we have changed the preview from a cube to a sphere. This will make it easier to see our changes.

That highlight looks a little strange for metal. It's too wide of a spot, which kind of makes it look like a soft plastic surface. We can adjust the sharpness of the highlight by plugging a constant into the **SpecularPower** input.

6. Create a new **Constant** node, give it a value of `100`, and plug it into **SpecularPower**. You'll see the highlight gets a lot sharper, though it's just as bright as it used to be.

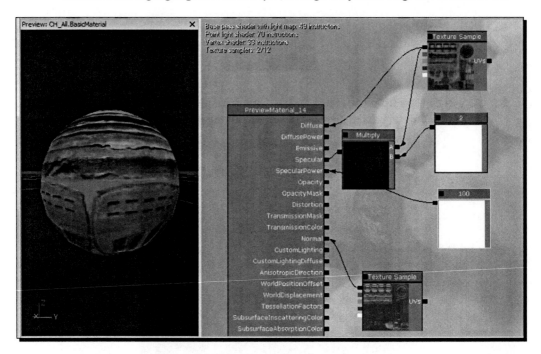

Play with the number and get a sense for the effect it has. Low numbers make the highlight really wide. High numbers make it sharper. Anything less than `1` looks kind of broken.

7. When you're happy with the results, hit the leftmost green checkmark to apply your changes, and check out your material in the scene.

8. Your network should now look as shown in the following screenshot:

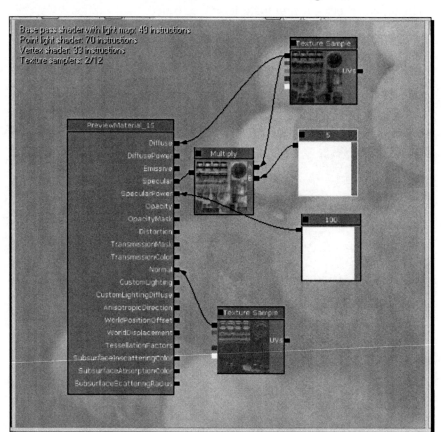

What just happened?

So, as you can see, the material is looking far better than before. How did we do this? As you can see from the image above, we now have 4 different types of mapping. We have the **Diffuse** map, **Specular** map, **SpecularPower** map, and a **Normal** map, which together have created a more realistic material for our environment, but were not finished yet. We are now going to look at color specular highlights.

Time for action – color specular highlight

Often times, reflections in metal take on a slightly bluish tone. So let's look at a new node type—a **Constant3Vector**, which is essentially a node that allows us to specify a color.

1. Click-and-drag a **Constant3Vector** into the **Material Editor** window. While a **Constant** has only one value that we can edit, a **Constant3Vector** has three values, **R**, **G**, and **B** (for red, green, and blue). By combining **R**, **G**, and **B**, we can make any color that your monitor can display.

2. Here you will see a box with R, G, B, and Desc options, and numbers opposite each option:

3. Type in a value of 1 for **R**; this will make the output of our node pure red. You can click the little black box at the top of the node to get a real-time. preview; notice the box turns yellow when the real-time preview is turned on.

4. Alright, let's hook this up to our specularity. We currently have a **Constant** multiplied against our texture. Let's replace it with this **Constant3Vector**.

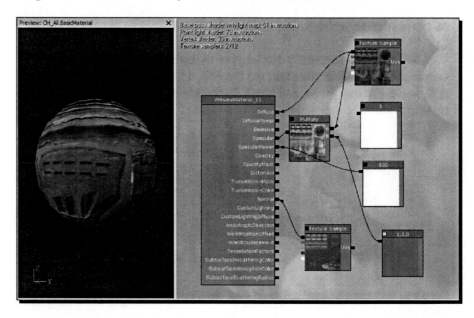

5. Ok, the highlight is definitely red, but it's pretty dim again. We could add another **Multiply** node and multiply in the **Constant**, but instead, we can just change the **R** value of the **Constant3Vector** to 5, and we'll get the same result.

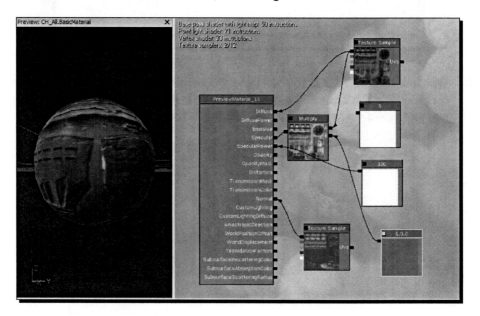

6. Now, all we need to do is pick a number for the **Constant3Vector** that looks good. I found 4, 4.5, or 5 looks good, but play with it yourself and come up with something you like. You can also delete that extra **Constant** node, since we're not using it anymore.

7. Your network should now look as shown in the following screenshot:

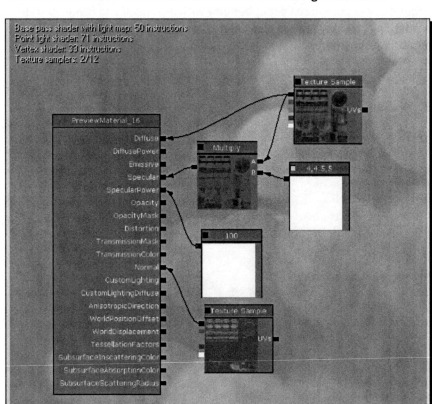

What just happened?

So, as you can see from the images above, the color specular highlight highlights certain areas of our material, making it look even more polished. So are there anymore tweaks that we can do; how about adding a tint to our **Diffuse Color** map.

Time for action – adding a tint to the diffuse color

Let's go through one more exercise, just to make sure you've got the basics. I won't walk you through it this time, but let's add a tint to the diffuse color.

1. Create a new **Multiply** node and a **Constant3Vector** node, and hook them up just like you did for the **Specular** color. Pick a nice rusty orange color for the tint (**1, 2**). You should end up with something that looks like the following screenshot:

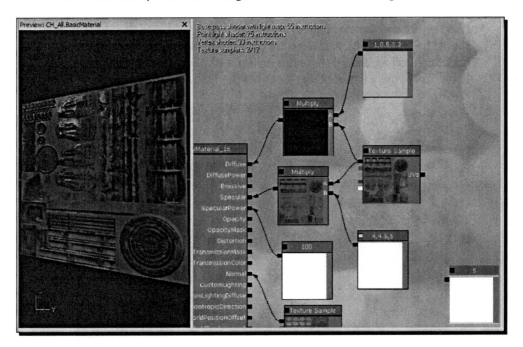

What just happened?

So, as you can see from the image above, we have added an orange tint diffuse color to our material, which is the finishing touch and now our material is ready to be used in our environment. The final section is to make our material easier to read in the **Material Editor**. So let's go ahead and polish things up.

Time for action – making your material easy to read

Almost over, but we've got one very important topic to cover—clean-up and commenting. You may be able to read your material just fine now, but when you come back in a week, or a month, an organized material with some useful comments will be a lot easier to understand.

1. The first step is good organization. As we've seen, data in the **Material Editor** flows right to left (the inputs of our nodes are on the right, and the spit out data to the left). Take some time now and organize your nodes so that there's no backtracking (the **Texture** and **Constant** nodes should be on the right, and the **Multiply** nodes should be to their left). Also organize things to minimize crisscrossing lines—the nodes controlling **Diffuse** should go on top, with the ones controlling **Specular** below. Try to get a network that looks like the following screenshot:

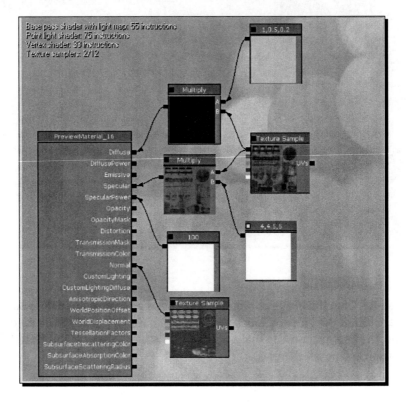

2. The next thing we can do to organize our network is label the nodes. For instance, what if you decided at some point that you didn't like the color of the **Specular** highlight? It would be a lot easier to figure out what to change, if that **Constant3Vector** node had a label on it. Select the node, and in the properties at the bottom, fill in the **Desc** field with a label for the node as **Specular Tint**.

3. The node now has text floating over it, saying what it does.

4. Label all of your input nodes this way. A good rule is, if it's a node you'd want to tune at some point (such as the **Texture** inputs and **Constant**), give it a label. If it's just a functional node (such as the **Multiply**), don't bother.

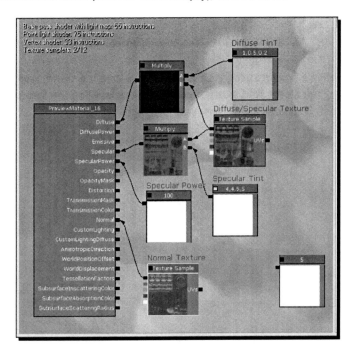

5. One more thing we can do is select a bunch of nodes and put a comment box around them. This groups them together in a logical way, and we can remind ourselves of what a whole cluster of nodes is supposed to achieve.

This network isn't really complex enough that comment boxes are critical, but let's add some anyway, so that you know how they work.

Select the **Diffuse Tint** node and the **Multiply** node it feeds into (*Ctrl*+click to select them, and right-click to add a comment box).

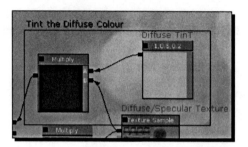

6. In the **Comment Text** window, add some useful text, such as `Tint the Diffuse`.

7. You now have a box grouping your nodes. If you drag it around, anything inside of it will be dragged along. Add another comment box labeling the **Specular Tint** nodes, hit the green checkmark, and save your package.

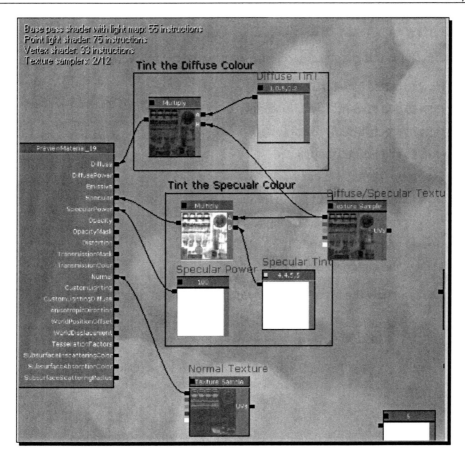

Believe it or not, this is an extremely powerful node network, and in fact does more than you need to produce a full-quality asset.

What just happened?

So, what we have done is added floating text underneath each map to show you what each one does, and that it doesn't get too confusing when you next create a new material.

Summary

We learned a lot in this chapter. Specifically, we covered the following:

- How to create a material
- How to add textures to our material
- How to create a shiny metal surface
- How to add normal mapping
- Seeing our material in our world
- How to use the perfect texture for our material
- How to create color specular highlights
- How to add a tint to our diffuse
- Making the material easy to read

So we have learnt how the **Material Editor** works, and how to create a material from scratch.

Pop Quiz Answers

Chapter 1

Level Design HQ

- **Left Mouse Button (LMB)**: Pan. right/left/forward/back movements
- **Right Mouse Button (RMB)**: Rotate, look around
- **LMB+RMB**: Up/down movements
- **WASD**: Movement hot keys

Chapter 2

Hello UDK

2. 2x1 Split

Chapter 3

Applying Lighting Effects

1. Point light
2. Spot light
3. Directional light
4. Sky light

Chapter 4

Battling the Elements

3. Area 3

Chapter 5

Movement with Movers

Kismet

Chapter 6

Terrain

1. Untouch
2. Objects
3. Double team
4. Disabler
5. Collision and lighting
6. Timing
7. Radios
8. Rewind
9. Untouch

Chapter 7

Adding Gameplay Elements into your Map

1. Deathmatch
2. Capture the flag
3. Vehicle capture the flag
4. Warfare

Index

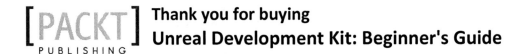

Thank you for buying
Unreal Development Kit: Beginner's Guide

About Packt Publishing

Packt, pronounced 'packed', published its first book "Mastering phpMyAdmin for Effective MySQL Management" in April 2004 and subsequently continued to specialize in publishing highly focused books on specific technologies and solutions.

Our books and publications share the experiences of your fellow IT professionals in adapting and customizing today's systems, applications, and frameworks. Our solution-based books give you the knowledge and power to customize the software and technologies you're using to get the job done. Packt books are more specific and less general than the IT books you have seen in the past. Our unique business model allows us to bring you more focused information, giving you more of what you need to know, and less of what you don't.

Packt is a modern, yet unique publishing company, which focuses on producing quality, cutting-edge books for communities of developers, administrators, and newbies alike. For more information, please visit our website: www.PacktPub.com.

Writing for Packt

We welcome all inquiries from people who are interested in authoring. Book proposals should be sent to author@packtpub.com. If your book idea is still at an early stage and you would like to discuss it first before writing a formal book proposal, contact us; one of our commissioning editors will get in touch with you.

We're not just looking for published authors; if you have strong technical skills but no writing experience, our experienced editors can help you develop a writing career, or simply get some additional reward for your expertise.

Unity 3D Game Development by Example Beginner's Guide

ISBN: 978-1-849690-54-6   Paperback:384 pages

A seat-of-your-pants manual for building fun, groovy little games quickly

1. Build fun games using the free Unity 3D game engine even if you've never coded before

2. Learn how to "skin" projects to make totally different games from the same file – more games, less effort!

3. Deploy your games to the Internet so that your friends and family can play them

4. Stay engaged with fresh, fun writing that keeps you awake as you learn

XNA 4.0 Game Development by Example: Beginner's Guide

ISBN: 978-1-849690-66-9   Paperback: 428 pages

Create exciting games with Microsoft XNA 4.0

1. Dive headfirst into game creation with XNA

2. Four different styles of games comprising a puzzler, a space shooter, a multi-axis shoot 'em up, and a jump-and-run platformer

3. Games that gradually increase in complexity to cover a wide variety of game development techniques

4. Focuses entirely on developing games with the free version of XNA

Please check **www.PacktPub.com** for information on our titles

Lightning Source UK Ltd.
Milton Keynes UK
UKOW021245090512

192217UK00003B/60/P